Contents

Praise for ENCOUNTER

Elizabeth's pinpoint precision on 90 days toward spiritual and emotional health points to a God-given alignment to loosing chains of fear, unforgiveness, anger and more. The things we assume are part of our personality are not—and this 90-day calendar journey is a fantastic and creative deep-dive to loosen these cords and run with the Lord toward freedom in identity! We are not our circumstances, but we are who HE says we are!

— **KATHI SMITH**, Senior Editor of The Healing Line at Christian Healing Ministries

Elizabeth's book will open your eyes to the power of renewing your mind with the Word of God. By the Spirit of God, she leads you on a path of how to replace thoughts of self defeat, rejection, and pain with thoughts of peace, love, and absolute victory in Christ! You will be blessed by this book and equipped to walk in your freedom in Christ.

— **ASHLEY ROBBINS,** God Within Her Ministries

ENCOUNTER

Your Personal Guidebook
for Inner Healing

ELIZABETH BOWMAN,
BCBC, ARS

HIGH BRIDGE BOOKS
HOUSTON

Encounter
by Elizabeth Bowman

Copyright © 2019 by Elizabeth Bowman
All rights reserved.

Printed in the United States of America
ISBN (Paperback): 978-1-946615-35-0

High Bridge Books titles may be purchased in bulk for educational, business, fundraising, or sales promotional use. For information please contact High Bridge Books via www.HighBridgeBooks.com/contact.

Published in Houston, Texas by High Bridge Books

Acknowledgments

I dedicate this book to Jesus, the Author and Perfecter of my faith, and to my husband, Chris, and my three children— Reid, Kenan and Olivia. We have traveled long distances and endured rocky roads together. We have stood, hands lifted high.

"I will go before you and level the exalted places, I will break in pieces the doors of bronze and cut through the bars of iron, I will give you the treasures of darkness and the hoards in secret places, that you may know that it is I, the LORD, the God of Israel, who call you by your name."

—Isaiah 45:2-3

Foreword

JESUS PROCLAIMS HE IS LIFE (Rom. 5:10). He invites us to live by faith, His faith, given to us as a free gift (Gal. 2:20). He demands there is only one work—to believe (John 6:28-29). He boldly states He will fight the battle for us. We are to be still (Exod. 14:14). Over and over, He encourages us to rest (Heb. 3 and 4) and abide (John 15). With the world, the patterns of our own flesh and the devil coming after us 24/7, how can we focus on the Way, His Life living through us (1 John 2:15-17)? Is it as simple as to believe, trust, and abide? Yes! However, it is not easy. Elizabeth gives us 90 opportunities to focus on Christ, the Truth, by working through our lie system that encourages flesh (Gal. 5:16-21). She gives insight on focusing on Christ and not the world's system of thinking. Instructions on how to "armor up" and "put on Christ" are laid out and made practical (Eph. 6 and Rom. 13:14).

This book is not a "fix-it," you'll-be-so-okay-that-you-won't-struggle-anymore manual. It is rendered as a way to focus on the problems that blind us to who we are and Who Christ is in our daily walk. It is an opportunity to embrace the Truth that we have everything we need to walk in life and godliness (2 Pet. 1:3), surrendering the obstacles to Christ by bringing the lies to Truth. As you work through the pages, there is an opening to understand how to oppose the world's thinking with Scriptural Truth and fight the good fight of faith against the enemy by understanding how we are giving him territory in our minds. Elizabeth teaches how to stand firm and encourages you that continuing to stand firm against the enemy's schemes brings us to the victory Christ has won for us (Eph. 6).

Engaging with God and consistently working through this manual will afford you an intimate relationship with Christ by removing the obstacles that keep you from running into the throne room of Grace crying, "Abba, Abba!" (Gal. 4:6). As freedom floods your heart, I invite you to do just that—run into His arms. This is the type of encounter whereby you experience intimacy with Christ. No one or no circumstance can ever take that from you!

—**RENÉE BERRY**, Discipleship Counselor, Life Coach, Teacher, Trainer, Consultant, Speaker, Author of *Invite Him In: Jesus in Seasons of Adversity*

Website: reneehberry.com
Email: renee@abundantgraceintl.org,
     rberry8609@gmail.com

Part One

Analyzing Thoughts

Encounter 1

Truth or Lies

ARE WE CAPABLE of telling ourselves the truth, or do we believe what circumstances try to tell us? Many times, when we look at our circumstances, they paint an entirely different picture than what is actually happening—both good and bad. However, it's quite amazing that human nature usually goes to the bad, which means we will believe the lie. Unfortunately, once we believe the first lie, it doesn't stop. The word of God is our source of ALL truth, and it is, in fact, the only source of infallible Truth.

Did you know that circumstances have a voice? These voices speak lies that come in like rushing water. They flood our minds and affect our heart. But how do we define *lies*? We can identify a lie by asking ourselves," Does this thought, feeling, or passion run contrary to what the Word of God says about me?" If so, it is a lie.

Can you think of something you believed at one time and discovered it wasn't what you initially thought? We all have. Afterward, we wonder, "Why was I so quick to believe it?" Usually, even when those first thoughts come, something within tries to tell us, "That can't be right!" Unfortunately, we don't always listen to that inner voice.

Write about a time when you knew better but believed the worst?

_____

_____

_____

_____

_____

How did you come to learn the truth?

_____

_____

_____

_____

_____

The Word tells us to cast *"down arguments and every high thing that exalts itself against the knowledge of God, bringing every thought into captivity to the obedience of Christ"* (2 Cor. 10:5 NKJV).

Today, I want to give you hope—hope that you *can* and *will* overcome such negative thinking, the belief that these lies are truth.

Prayer: Thank You, Lord, that I hear Your voice and learn to lean upon You for clarity and wisdom. Thank You for healing my mind and bringing my emotions in line with the truth. I am fearfully and wonderfully made in Your image, and I am loved because I am Your child. Amen.

Encounter 2

Rejection

HOW OFTEN DO WE go through trials where rejection plays a primary role? Rejection is a false belief that can cause us to think negative thoughts about ourselves, God, and others. More often than we would like to admit, rejection bleeds feelings of inferiority and unworthiness. If we allow rejection to take root and become our core belief, we can react out of *fear, jealousy,* and *"self-preservation,"* which can cause our emotions to rage. Can you remember a time when you felt this way?

Emotions such as anger, fear, and control can cause us to lash out and react out of this place of deep hurt.

When this happens, do you feel rejected even by God? Why?

_____

_____

_____

_____

_____

When triggered by these negative, seemingly unfair, external circumstances, do you want to blame others, including God, as your defense mechanism?

_____

_____

_____

_____

_____

Our defense mechanism of blame is exactly the enemy's plans. But this should be the first clue that we need to take every thought captive. Instead of complaining, we should give thanks. What? Give thanks? How can I give thanks when everything is coming against me? The Bible says in 1 Thessalonians 5:18, *"In everything give thanks; for this is the will of God in Christ Jesus for you."* We don't give thanks for the circumstances, but we give thanks that we have a God Who loves us. Yes, God loves you. You are His child. The Word also says, *"Be strong and of good courage, do not fear nor be afraid of **them**; for the Lord your God, **He is the One who goes with you. He will not leave you nor forsake you**"* (Deut. 31:6).

So, in every situation, when negative thoughts and emotions try to rise up, now you know what your response will be.

Prayer: Thank You, God, that You are with me. You love me and have not rejected me. You go where I go. You have great plans for me, not to harm me but to give me a great future. I love You and thank You for turning all things for good in my life. I am and will overcome every circumstance in the Name of Jesus, Amen.

Encounter 3

Trusting God

SEASONS OF DIFFICULTY can come at us. Maybe you've been in a dry season for quite some time. These are the times we want answers. But everyone, including the Lord, went through unfair, trying times. We are called to live a selfless life. Staying focused on self, asking such as "why me," can lead us into grief, depression, anger, and bitterness. The root of bitterness defiles our progress for the Lord (Hebrews 12:15). Instead we must stay focused on Jesus and *all* that He has done for us. He always leads us to greater freedom and joy.

No matter what, He promises to work all things together for the good of those who love Him (Rom. 8:28). It may not seem that anything good or positive could come from our valley experience, but its sole purpose is to transform us.

Are you willing to be transformed by God?

_____

_____

_____

_____

_____

_____

_____

How will you respond to His transformation for your life and for His glory?

_____

_____

_____

_____

_____

_____

_____

When you allow Jesus Christ to transform you in the fire, He will change you from reacting in fear to responding in love, from believing the enemy's lies to following the truth of His Word. It may not seem easy in the beginning, but when you learn to follow His ways, you will soon discover that it is good that His ways are higher than ours. We will also learn that we can trust Him because He loves us so much.

Today, let us decide to let Him rule in our lives—to trust Him in all things.

Prayer: Father, thank You for Your gracious, never-ending love for me. Please forgive me for trying to be in charge. Even when I don't understand or agree, I know I am free to ask "Why," but instead I will trust You in every area of my life. I will continue to thank You for Your wisdom and plan, knowing that You are working and wanting to do Your good pleasure in my life. I will follow You, in Jesus' Name. Amen.

Encounter 4

Being Renewed

THE BIBLE TELLS US in Ephesians 4: 21–24 to *"put off"* old patterns of belief systems and, instead, to *"put on"* new ways of thinking.

> *If indeed you have heard Him and have been taught by Him, as the truth is in Jesus: that you put off, concerning your former conduct, the old man which grows corrupt according to the deceitful lusts, and be renewed in the spirit of your mind, and that you put on the new man which was created according to God, in true righteousness and holiness.* (Eph. 4:21–24)

Will you consider making the change? This is a process! It takes time to begin to look inward and address the real root issues of the heart and the mind. When we became born again, our mind did not get a "makeover." We can still have a lot of emotional baggage and wrong habits clogging up our mind. Our spirit (heart) became an entirely new creation with the life and nature of God in it, but as a born-again, believer our minds need a "makeover" too because it is used to its old pattern of thinking. We need to get a brand-new way of living and thinking. How? Well, to start, allow me to ask you these questions:

What thoughts invade your mind? Are they fear/anxiety-based?

_____

_____

_____

_____

_____

If you have negative thoughts, do you also feel it in your body?

_____

_____

_____

_____

Do you experience this daily?

_____

_____

_____

_____

Are you willing to change these negative patterns and replace them with positive words?

_____

_____

_____

_____

Read the above Scripture again. Allow His words to penetrate your heart. Sit for the next five minutes and speak those words over yourself.

Prayer: Father, thank You today for teaching me to realize when my thoughts line up with the world and when they line up with You. I want to follow You only, walk in the truth, and be renewed in my mind. Thank You for being there for me and helping me in and out of times of trouble. Your ways are higher than mine, and Your thoughts are higher than mine. I desire to follow You in every area of my life. In Jesus' Name, Amen

Encounter 5

The Process

PERHAPS AS YOU BEGIN this journey of renewing your mind and changing negative thought patterns, you find yourself thinking, "This adjustment is hard. Why is it not easier? Why am I having such a hard time?" The antidote comes in Matthew 11:30 where Jesus says, "The Truth is my yoke is easy and my burden is light."

We focus on how hard it is, but we need to shift our focus on Jesus' yoke, which is easy. If you are willing to do things a new way—His Way—, it's going to take discipline. It's a process. It takes time. You've got to be willing, and then be patient with yourself. It's not always easy. However, to successfully align our thoughts with His requires spending time in His Word—reading and studying it on a consistent basis. His Word is the light unto our path. God is faithful, and once you start your new journey, you will find Him to be the ever-present help He promises us to be.

> "God is our refuge and strength,
> A very present help in trouble" (Ps. 46:1).

Have you ever planted a garden? If you have, you know there is a process. You must first prepare the ground. The soil has to be tilled, and then you can plant the seeds. It may require daily watering at first, but it needs constant attention.

Our hearts also have layers and areas that need daily attention. For example, we may have layers of bitterness and forgiveness that we need to be willing to till and allow His dark, rich soil to impact our wounded hearts. His soil is the Word, and His presence in us will accomplish the beautiful end result—being transformed for His glory.

What is your pattern of living?

_____

_____

_____

_____

Are you disciplined?

_____

_____

_____

_____

What areas do you need to submit to Him for restructuring?

_____

_____

_____

_____

Take some time and visualize the "new garden" you'd like to see growing up in your life. Write out what you want your garden to look like.

_____

_____

_____

_____

Prayer: Father, we thank You this adjustment is light and easy for me because you said your "yoke is easy and your burden is light." At times, it can feel painful on the flesh, but with my heart and mind, I stay focused on the Word. Today thank you for preparing us to look like You. We want to have an open heart to receive our healing in every area. Let Your light shine in my life revealing the hidden places, so I will bloom and be an example to others. I want to be disciplined so I can be whole in Jesus' Name. Amen.

Encounter 6

Perseverance

IF WE ARE GOING to *"put off"* old patterns of belief systems and *"put on"* new ways of thinking, it will require discipline and perseverance. In Oswald Chambers' *My Utmost for His Highest,* we glimpse a new way of living:

> *Perseverance is more than endurance. It is endurance combined with absolute assurance and certainty that what we are looking for is going to happen. Perseverance means more than just hanging on, which may be only exposing our fear of letting go and falling.*

There is so much to hope for in life, especially a life with the Lord. However, perseverance only works when we are assured of the outcome—that it will be a wonderful change for the better. The Apostle Paul tells us to *"be renewed in the spirit of your mind."* So, how does one renew their mind?

Have you ever had to persevere? If so, write down your experience. How did you make it through?

_____

_____

_____

_____

_____

Can you recall a shift in your thinking? Did anything inside you change?

_____

_____

_____

_____

_____

Has fear ever tried to stop you from moving forward? If so, can you recall how you persevered?

_____

_____

_____

_____

_____

The question here is, are we afraid of letting go as Mr. Chambers suggests? Fear is not from God; when we start to feel this emotion, we must first stop and change our thinking. By quoting the Word, the truth, and coming into agreement with the Holy Spirit, fear will leave. This is how your mind is renewed. This is the work of the Holy Spirit.

Prayer: Father, I thank You for the plan You have for my life. I know I can do all things through Christ Who strengthens me because Your Word tells me I can. I will not be afraid of letting go of past thoughts or emotions that don't line up with Your Word. I won't be afraid I can't change. Even though I am struggling and in a difficult place right now, I _choose You_ and purpose to _persevere_ to _victory_ in You. Amen.

Encounter 7

Being Transformed

WILL YOU ALLOW God to refine you? In your deepest, darkest valley—when your circumstances are anything but good—you still get to choose! So, will you run toward Him, or will you run away? We must believe that we have choices; we can either respond or react.

In our mind, we may experience overwhelming emotions like anxiety, worry, jealousy, anger, covetousness, bitterness, comparison, etc. These emotions leave us isolated, rejected, empty, and lonely. However, when we choose His ways, the outcome is joy, peace, rest, longsuffering, and patience. Will you believe that while you are in your brokenness, He is making you beautiful?

Everyone goes through hard times—trials and times of testing—designed to transform us into the image of Christ.

What does the word *transform* mean to you?

_____

_____

_____

_____

_____

Do you remember a time of trying/testing that transformed you for your good?

_____

_____

_____

_____

_____

How did you encounter God in a new and refreshing way?

_____

_____

_____

_____

The Word tells us that regardless of the situation we have to go through, sometimes even when it's our own doing, God will always use our situations, circumstances, and relationships for our good in making and molding us into the image of Christ. Romans 8:28 tells us,

> And we know that all things work together for good to those who love God, to those who are the called according to His purpose.

Prayer: Father, we thank You for watching over us, leading us in the way we should go. Help me to trust You and Your ways as I am being transformed into the image and Christ-likeness of Your dear Son, Jesus. I want to be willing to let You lead me in every area of my life. Your Word is the truth, and I will be transformed as I allow it to change my old ways and thoughts, in Jesus' Name, Amen.

Encounter 8

All Things Are Made New

THE APOSTLE PAUL instructs us to,

> ... *Fix your thoughts on what is true, and honorable, and right, and pure, and lovely, and admirable. Think about things that are excellent and worthy of praise.* (Phil. 4:8)

This is where you will find that Jesus is alive in the midst of the fiery trial and in your deepest suffering. You can choose to believe that, regardless of your trial, Jesus will take you to a higher place so that you will really get to know Him and bring glory and honor to His Name.

I learned this myself during a season of spiritual famine and dryness. However, since then, the Lord has made *all things new.* He has come alive in a more intimate way, deep in the core of my being, my spirit, and my mind! In the valley, He meets me and allows me to find true joy—to dance.

In what areas would you like to see "all things made new" in your life?

_____

_____

_____

_____

_____

Are you willing to exchange the negative thoughts for the positive thoughts as Paul admonishes?

_____

_____

_____

Give an example of a new way of thinking about one of your current issues.

Example: I'm never going to be able to have my own business.

*I can do all things through Christ Who strengthens me!

_____

_____

_____

_____

God's plan for us never changes. He wants us to be relating more intimately to Him, regardless of the outcome. He can make all things new. The change comes when I focus on Him and not my circumstance. It's not too late. Let today be your day to begin fresh with the Lord and His Word.

Prayer: Lord, I pray that as I make the choice to press out old patterns, behaviors, and beliefs that keep me from Your presence, walls of pride and the lies that invade my heart will come down. Your truth, light, and love will fill me. Thank You for what You will do and are doing in my life! All things will be made new in the Name of Jesus, my Savior and Lord, Amen!

Encounter 9

Receiving Him

GOD'S PLAN FROM THE BEGINNING was relationship! At no time did God expect us to do life alone. From the very beginning, He created mankind, Adam and Eve, to fellowship with Him. The Word states that He came down every day to spend time with them in the Garden (Gen. 3:8).

Now we know all this changed when they sinned. However, His plan to spend time with us has not changed. This was His purpose in sending His Son—to restore us back to our original relationship with Him. The question is if we allow time to be with Him and experience His presence.

Do you take time to read His Word?

_____

_____

_____

_____

Do you pray?

_____

_____

_____

_____

Do you wait on Him during these times to give you specific instructions?

_____

_____

_____

_____

Do you write down what He says to you?

_____

_____

_____

_____

It's hard to believe that an Almighty God would want to spend time with us, especially when we know how wrong or how bad we've been. However, His Word declares,

> Let your conduct be without covetousness; be content with such things as you have. For He Himself has said, "I will never leave you nor forsake you"' So, we may boldly say: "The Lord is my helper; I will not fear. What can man do to me?" (Heb. 13:5–6).

Prayer: Thank you, Lord, that You are with me. You are leading me and guiding me so I can follow You and Your ways with confidence, that I will be renewed and transformed to follow Your plan for my life. I will take time to be with You. I do hear Your voice. I will be made completely whole. Amen

Encounter 10

Applying Truth

RENEWING AND TRANSFORMING our minds is easier than you think. The bottom line is being able to recognize who is doing the talking and changing the negative, worldly way of thinking with the only truth, which is the Word of God.

If you are having a hard time trusting Jesus, because your eyes are on your outcome, turn your focus to Jesus. His Living Word will light the path as you begin to seek Him in your current situation.

> *Now faith is the substance of things hoped for, the evidence of things not seen.* (Heb. 11:1)

> *For as he thinks in his heart, so is he.* (Prov. 23:7)

> *God's Word is able to do the work that is needed. All the issues of your life are changed by getting a new belief system.* (Heb. 4:12)

> *Finally, brethren, whatever things are true, whatever things are honest, whatever things are just, whatever things being pure, whatever things are lovely, whatever things are of good report; if there is any virtue, and if there is any praise, think on these things. Those things, which ye have both learned, and received, and heard, and seen in me, do: and the God of peace will be with you.* (Phil. 4:8, 9 WBT)

Quoting the Word is essential to keeping our thoughts aligned with God's plan. Four actions you can take that will keep you focused on Jesus are:

Visualize the victory
Speak the Word—the Truth
Speak the Word with authority and power
Pray and believe you have received

This brings a knowing of Jesus and Who He is for you in the battle. He is our Peace.

Prayer: Father, we thank You for the plan You have for our lives. Thank You that I can trust You because Your Word is truth, and it declares that You work to will Your good pleasure in my life. Help me to always believe the truth of Your Word instead of any lies with negative emotions. It's Your truth that really does set me free. Thank You!

Encounter 11

Building Faith

THE BIBLE SAYS in Romans 10:17,

> *So, then faith comes by hearing, and hearing by the word of God.*

If we want to see victory when the trials begin, we need God's help. This means we must use faith by trusting. The Word tells us it's faith that pleases God (Heb. 11:6), and faith without works is dead (Jas. 2:26). So how do we build our faith? It comes by trusting the Holy Spirit to illumine our hearing, quoting and memorizing the Living Word.

What areas do you need changes in?

_____

_____

_____

_____

_____

_____

What Bible verses will you speak over yourself on a daily basis?

_____

_____

_____

_____
_____
_____
_____

What expectations do you visualize?

_____
_____
_____
_____
_____

When we use God's Word over our circumstances, we cannot fail. The Word says it does not come back void. In other words, it will accomplish what it's designed to do. That's why this action is so important. It puts faith to work, which pleases God.

Prayer: Thank You, Lord, that faith comes by hearing the Word of God. As I speak Your Word, my trust will increase my faith. Thank you for renewing my mind to hear Your voice—the truth—in every situation. The Bible says Your ways and Your thoughts are higher than mine. Thank You that I can trust You, even when I don't understand or agree. I am Your child; You love me. I will be victorious in You! Thank You. Amen.

Encounter 12

Living by Faith

MANY YEARS AGO, a friend told me about a conversation she had with the Lord. He was teaching her how to have great faith. There are only three places in the Bible where Jesus commended the individual for having great faith. Amazingly, these individuals weren't even what we would call Christians.

The first was the Roman Centurion who came and asked Jesus to heal his servant. When Jesus replied, "I'll come to your house," the man replied, "That's not necessary. Just say the word, and it will be done." Think about it! Who wouldn't want Jesus to come to their house? I would. But this man understood the power in the Word ... "The Word became flesh and dwelt among them" (John 1:14). Can you see why Jesus said he had great faith?

We must ask ourselves whether we have great faith? Do we see the Word of God, even today, as Jesus in the flesh talking with us, instructing us, delivering us, and healing us? Do we believe? And if we believe, are we using His *Word* to live by faith?

How would you answer that question today?

_____

_____

_____

Do you use the Word over your circumstances like it is the weapon it was created to be?

_____

_____

_____

Give an example of a verse or verses you use on a daily basis.

_____

_____

_____

One of the daily Words I use to strengthen my faith is from Isaiah 54:17, "No weapon formed against me shall prosper." This verse brings me great comfort in knowing that nothing can ever hurt me. And "no thing" can ever hurt you, either.

Prayer: Father, thank You for sending Your Son, who became flesh and lives among us. As a part of great faith, living intimately with you, I know when I speak Your Word daily, I am living by faith, counting on You to perform Your Word in my life. Thank You that Your Word never returns void. I can expect victory when I use it. Glory be to God. Amen.

Encounter 13

Decisions

WHAT DOES IT TAKE to finally come to a place in our life where we understand the need to make a change—and the need to do it now? This isn't a minor change like going on a diet or choosing to exercise, although, if these issues are causing you major health concerns, then they are necessary.

However, one major decision we all should make is to respond to the Holy Spirit's call to receive Jesus Christ, God's Son, as our Savior. When you do this, the Word says you have a new nature. You have put on Christ. You have become a new creation. 2 Corinthians 5:17 says, *"Old things have passed away, and all things are become new."* Our inner self rejoices. We are now born again.

The most encouraging thing for all of us, especially if we have made some serious mistakes in our lives, is the comfort in knowing that we are forgiven and made brand new. The past literally doesn't exist. Isn't this good news?

What is the first thing you need to make a decision about?

_____

_____

_____

What is your plan of action to help you stay focused on your decision?

_____

_____

_____

_____

_____

By staying focused on Jesus, new habits can be created. This is the first step in changing anything about ourselves. Let this be day 1 of your new beginning. Even if you have already accepted Christ as Your Savior and Lord, you know there are some things you need to *decide* to change. Because of your union with Christ and the leading of the Holy Spirit, you "can do all things through Christ Who strengthens" you." (Phil. 4:13). If you haven't accepted Him, let today be your day. Just ask the Father to forgive you of your sins and ask Jesus to come into your heart as your Savior and Lord. Both requests will be answered immediately, and you will be born again.

Prayer: Father, I thank You that my old nature has passed away. Help me stay on Your path, following Your ways. I want my decisions to be Your decisions. I choose You to be my guide! I know if I follow You and Your Word, I will achieve victory in every area of my life. Thank You for loving me and creating an excellent plan for my life.

Encounter 14

Staying the Course

Have you ever tried to go on a diet or plan a daily routine change only to fall back into the old pattern within a short time? For a while, we feel like we have it made, but then the fleshly lies from the past flex their muscles again. We thought we were going in a new direction—walking on God's path to a life of righteous living, but we discover that our flesh is at war with this new creation. You want to change directions—change your behavior—but how do you do this, when it seems so hard to do?

Dr. Mark Shaw writes in his book, *The Heart of Addiction*:

> Physical addiction occurs when you repeatedly satisfy a natural appetite/desire with a temporary pleasure ... Addiction is likened to slavery and idolatry in the Bible. You use a temporarily pleasurable substance to escape, but in reality, you find that you are physically enslaved rather than free. (Shaw 2009, 27)

The first thing we must do is be honest with ourselves. We will never be able to change our direction and make good decisions without being truthful about who and where we really are in our walk with the Lord. Take inventory of your thoughts, reconsider if necessary, and then take action over what enslaves you.

What area(s) would you like to change?

_____

_____

_____

_____

_____

What is your course of action to achieve this?

_____

_____

_____

_____

_____

The key to successfully making changes in any area is to trust in the Lord's ability to do it. He alone is the truth and the way. Lean on Him!

Prayer: Father, I thank You today that You are faithful. You love me and have great plans for me, which I will fulfill in Jesus' Name. I can do all things through You, and I can change old patterns and habits to line up with Your Word and the future You have already prepared for me. Thank You again for not giving up on me. You are always with me—what a comfort and relief.

Encounter 15

Right Thinking

NO ONE EVER SAID it was easy to change an old habit or a destructive behavioral pattern in one's life. Even the Apostle Paul faced challenges. Notice what he wrote to the Roman church:

> *Although I have the desire to do what is right, I don't do it. I don't do the good I want to do. Instead, I do the evil that I don't want to do. Now, when I do what I don't want to do, I am no longer the one who is doing it. Sin that lives in me is doing it ... Who will rescue me from my dying body. I thank God that our Lord Jesus Christ rescues me!* (Rom. 7:18–20; 23–26)

Little by little, we change and grow. Only God knows why it seems to take us so long to reflect Christ, think godly thoughts, speak with wisdom, and live a life by faith. Maybe you, like so many Christians, are still bound in some area of your life.

Is there something you feel is managing you instead of you managing it? What needs to be released to God?

_____

_____

_____

Does the temporary pleasure lead you to be stuck in a negative pattern of guilt and shame?

_____

_____

_____

Do you have a plan to change it? What is your plan?

_____

_____

_____

_____

Making the decision to change is always the first step. The only delivering power there is comes from the Lord. The next time the temptation arises, have your new plan ready to implement, a new way of thinking. You can do all things through Christ. The Word says you have the mind of Christ, which means you can think right! Plus, you know He will help you.

Prayer: Thank You, Lord, that You have a great plan for my life. Your ways are higher than mine, so I can trust You to bring peace and relief without any outside influence. You can fulfill my every desire. You know me better than I do— You created me. I trust You to fill me with Your thoughts so that I think right and can prosper in areas that have kept me defeated in the past. I am new in You! Amen!

Encounter 16

Forming Habits

OUR FAMILY LOVES to go to the beach! Years ago, it took us over four and a half hours to get to the beach because the roads from our home to the coast were a combination of two-lane roads, a four-lane highway, and an interstate. We were able to drive a little faster on the four-lane highway, and we made really good time on the interstate. Faster is better, right?

With fewer exits, faster speed limits, and fewer interruptions, this was a faster way to get to our destination. However, is faster always better? At first, you might think so, but some things are worth the wait. Think about how hard it is to even build an interstate highway or a new and wider road. Both are time-consuming, but if you are making the journey on a regular basis, it is well worth the wait.

This is how it is with habits. Making changes takes work. It takes time and patience, which isn't today's main method of operation. However, most of us would admit to the need to make changes, and we know when it's time to do so.

Are you ready to admit you have chosen the wrong road or path?

_____

_____

_____

What habits are you willing to change?

_____

_____

_____

_____

_____

How will you go about changing them?

_____

_____

_____

_____

Don't be afraid. God will be with you. Don't let the enemy lie and tell you, "It's been too long!" Maybe you hear, "That's the way it is in your family ... your mom did it ... your dad did it, etc." Yes, maybe they did have issues, but you are uniquely created. You are a new person—old things are passed away. This is the truth, and the Word says, "The truth will set you free."

Prayer: Thank You, Lord, that I am free indeed because of Your blood. I can do all things through You. I am an overcomer, and I will be victorious in this plan to make changes and follow Your Word. Amen!

Encounter 17

Finding a Balance

MANY TIMES, WE KNOW we need to make changes but just aren't quite sure where to start. Maybe you're the kind of person who makes 25 New Year's resolutions every year.

This is frustrating and can lead to false expectations. Within a short while, you have no motivation to do anything toward your new goals at all. So, what's the answer? One day at a time, with your focus on Jesus! When He taught the disciples how to pray, He said, "Give us this day our daily bread." It would have been nice if He'd said monthly bread or yearly bread, but He didn't. We also know He wasn't just talking about food here. He was referring to our daily needs/supply.

This is why it's important to spend time with Him in the beginning to get "His" plan. We may know some things, but He knows everything, and He knows us better than we know ourselves. His "daily" plan keeps us balanced and motivated to keep moving forward.

Have you asked Him how to overcome your problem area?

_____

_____

_____

Why or why not?

_____

_____

_____

_____

_____

Do you have His daily plan?

_____

_____

_____

_____

_____

If you haven't asked Him for guidance, why not? Many times, we don't want to ask because of fear—fear that we won't hear Him—fear that He doesn't care. However, the Word says, *"You have not because you ask not"* (Jas. 4:3). Make it your first plan to ask Him—then follow His plan.

Prayer: Lord, I know there are areas where I need to go in a new direction. I'm willing to give up this path (routine) to follow Your ways. I know they are so much better for me. I will ask You for Your direction. I want to succeed, and I thank You for leading me down the path I should take. I will change because You are with me, leading me and guiding me. Thank You. In Jesus' Name. Amen!

Encounter 18

The Beaten Path

HAVE YOU EVER WONDERED where the phrase "the beaten path" came from? It could just mean it's a popular path that everyone takes because it's the shortest, fastest route. Maybe it means it's an older path that has had many travelers over the years. But what if it means it's the path that has been abused, neglected, or forgotten?

These are the hardest paths to get off of, to make positive changes, to choose a better way or direction to go. It's hard because of the habits that develop from these circumstances. Habits are like the roads or pathways we choose to take. It takes a while to form a habit—whether positive or negative. We get used to going the same way, creating a steady routine, which makes us think this is easier, less painful. However, even though we arrive at our destination, is this really the best route or have we become numb—no longer aware of where this road is leading us?

Have you gone down the road of abuse, neglect, or abandonment?

_____

_____

_____

_____

_____

Do you believe things can change?

_____

_____

_____

_____

_____

What do you see as your biggest hindrance?

_____

_____

_____

_____

_____

These paths or roads are like our brain. Once the pathway has been created, it can be difficult to change. The good news is that our brain can regenerate itself and form new pathways of healthy habits by taking our thoughts captive, thinking on things that are lovely, taking action, and renewing our minds. This is the instruction God gives us in His Word. When you accept that you are a child of the Most High God, your worth and value change. No, it may not be an immediate, overnight change, but it will change—you will be changed.

Prayer: Father, I thank You that I am Your child. You do love me unconditionally. My worth is in Your Son, Jesus, Who said He would never leave me or forsake me. Thank You that by walking in truth I can receive all that is necessary to become the person You intended for me to be, whole and free in every area. Amen.

Encounter 19

Taking Inventory

CHANGING OUR PATTERNS of thinking and our daily routines may seem to be overwhelming—maybe not even possible. But once you establish a relationship with the Lord, you will discover that some things are easier than you thought. The first step in any action is the same—you have to begin!

The way to begin your new path is to take inventory of your thoughts. Reconsider your thoughts, if necessary, and then take action over what enslaves you. The Lord is faithful to always bring light to the areas in our lives that He wants to refine. The end result will make our journey more fulfilling and full of joy.

What thoughts still try to consume most of your time?

_____

_____

_____

_____

_____

Did you know that for every negative, defeating thought, the Word has the exact opposite promise?

For example: I'm too scared to try anything new.

For God doesn't give us a spirit of fear, but of power, and of love, and a sound mind. (2 Tim. 1:7)

_____
_____
_____
_____
_____

The enemy continues to lie to us, especially if he thinks he can get away with it. Remember, what he says will contain some truth. If I had on a red shirt, he wouldn't try to tell me it was blue, but he could try to steal my self-worth by telling me that red has never been my color and makes me look fat. Now if this is what I said to myself, would I just change my shirt or would I feel bad about how I looked? I think we all know the answer to that question.

The truth is, the Word says, *"The enemy comes to kill, steal and destroy"* (John 10:10). But it also says, *"I [Christ] came to give [us] life and life more abundantly."* Remember, the Word says, *"As a man thinks in his heart, so is he."* (Prov. 23:7), so let's submit to the Truth so our thinking patterns will line up with the Word, and we can receive His abundant Life.

Prayer: Thank You, Father, that Your plan from the very beginning was to give us abundant life, Jesus. Help me recognize when destructive thoughts are trying to manipulate my thinking so I can replace them with Your Word. I can choose to change my thinking. Thank You, Lord. Amen.

Encounter 20

Finding Hope

I had many crooked paths and habits that had formed over the years. At times, because of wrong thinking, I repeatedly did the same thing, which led me to physical and mental exhaustion, even depression. I knew in order to change, I needed to be willing to be humble, surrender my pride, and allow Him to search my heart. I am still a work in progress, but I have found freedom in building the road His way. I am also glad that this new road, a road less traveled, leads to hope, restoration, love, and freedom.

We can't do this on our own, by the way. We need the Lord to live His life through us. I received Him as Life and you can too by fully depending on Him. Study Paul's words to the Roman church:

> So here's what I want you to do, God helping you: Take your everyday, ordinary life—your sleeping, eating, going-to-work, and walking-around life—and place it before God as an offering. Embracing what God does for you is the best thing you can do for him. Don't become so well-adjusted to your culture that you fit into it without even thinking. Instead, fix your attention on God. You'll be changed from the inside out. Readily recognize what he wants from you, and quickly respond to it. Unlike the culture around you, always dragging you down to its level of immaturity,

God brings the best out of you, develops well-formed maturity in you. (Rom. 12:1–2 MSG)

Are you willing to place your everyday routine/habits before the Lord for examination?

_____

_____

_____

_____

What are the key areas you need to surrender to Him?

_____

_____

_____

_____

What do you see as your biggest hindrance in keeping you from receiving from Him?

_____

_____

_____

_____

Even if you have tried to surrender these areas in the past and failed, don't be afraid to let go and let Him take charge. He can and will help you succeed.

Prayer: Father God, this battle is hard at times. Sometimes it feels safer to stay with the old, even though it's only a temporary fix that ultimately leaves me exhausted and sad. Thank You for showing me Your ways and helping me form new habits that lead to finding hope and joy in You. Amen.

Encounter 21

Peace

WHAT IF, when the storms come and the waves rage, you grab your Bible and meditate on the Word? Have you tried this? I assure you it works. In fact, the Word declares that it will not return void. This means it will do what it says it will do.

One Scripture we could focus on during these times of turmoil is,

"Peace, be still!" (Mark 4:39)

Do you believe that His Word can help you have peace in the midst of the storm? Yes, it still takes faith to believe this to be true. However, faith is what changes things. The enemy wants to convince you that all is lost and there is nothing you can do. However, he is the father of lies. The truth is that you can change things. You can believe God and His Word and use faith as a result of that belief to receive His peace. When we use faith and speak God's Word—His promises—it eliminates fear, which is the emotion that usually tries to accompany stress and traumatic events.

Do you believe it's possible for peace to reign over fear in your life?

_____

_____

_____

_____

_____

_____

What action are you willing to take now to overcome your trials?

_____

_____

_____

_____

_____

_____

What if you were willing to meet each obstacle that appeared on the horizon of your daily life with a steadfastness, a determined choice to focus the very core of your being on His command to be still? Maybe this is the key to how we receive Him as our Peace—we need to be still.

Prayer: Father, thank You for Your Word that encourages and brings hope and peace when I am troubled. You know every situation I'm going through and every thought I'm thinking. I believe and trust in Your plan for me, regardless of what it looks like right now. Help me to be still so I can hear Your voice. Forgive me. I want to trust You, and I will receive Your peace, joy, and love for me. Amen.

Encounter 22

Fear or Faith?

In John 16:33 we read,

I have said these things to you, that in me you may have peace. In the world you will have tribulation. But take heart; I have overcome the world.

Herein lies the biblical answer for when we face the storms of life. Even as these storms approach, and certainly they will, we need to recognize them for what they are, and through agreeing with Jesus our mind is renewed. We can receive a place of true and sincere peace. Why is this so important? The obvious reason is our physical health. Medical science has proven that negative emotions cause all kinds of diseases and ailments to the natural body. However, love destroys fear, which is the enemy's number one weapon. The enemy motivates people through fear, but God motivates us through His love.

Fear is the first negative emotion that existed on Planet Earth. It came about as the result of Adam and Eve's sin. The Word tells us as soon as they ate the forbidden fruit, they immediately hid because they were afraid of God.

When debilitating fear has come against me, I have submersed myself in scriptures that minister to me about God's love for me. 1 Corinthians 13 and 1 John 4:18 are two examples of God's love for us. What about these scriptures speaks to your heart?

_____

_____

_____

When you use His Word during your own fearful times, did you see things change? If so, can you explain what shifted for you?

_____

_____

_____

What Scripture do you need to quote even now as you trust Jesus to see victory in your life?

_____

_____

_____

_____

_____

We can't operate in both faith and fear at the same time. The only way to remove fear and stay in faith is to quote the Word, trust in the Lord, and pray. I know this may sound simple, but once you see God work when you do this, you won't stop it. He is faithful to accomplish what He sent His Word to do (Jer. 1:12).

Prayer: Father, I thank You for loving me and giving me the ability to overcome fear. I choose to walk in faith and trust in You. I rebuke fear and receive Your love in every area of my life. With You, I will be victorious and live in faith. In Jesus' Precious Name, Amen!

Encounter 23

God's Plan

I BELIEVE THAT once your storms pass, you will be left with a unique set of eclectic shells that have surfaced. These may be shells of amazing gifts that have been buried deep within your being ... shells that have finally awakened parts or even all of your body that has been sleeping for far too long ... shells of hope, of peace, of the expectation that God has a *good plan* for your life.

Nothing happens to us without the Lord seeing, knowing, understanding, and bringing loveliness and purpose out of the trial. He has expressly designed shells just for your journey — shells that tell an amazing story of God's love and care in the midst of the trial of your faith. You will also discover others in your sphere of influence who will need your shell!

As you trust Jesus have you been able to experience Him as your Prince of Peace in your storm?

_____

_____

_____

_____

_____

_____

Do you believe that God has a good plan for you? How have you seen His plan come to pass in your situation?

_____

_____

_____

_____

_____

_____

Can you trust Christ for future events? Why or Why not?

_____

_____

_____

_____

_____

God has a plan for you, a good plan. All you have to do is accept it, believe it, and receive it! He is a good God Who loves you very much. Peter 1:7 says,

> *That the trial of your faith, being much more precious than of gold that perisheth, though it be tried with fire, might be found unto praise and honour and glory at the appearing of Jesus Christ.*

Prayer: Father, I believe and trust that You have a good plan for my life. I receive You plan and love. I declare that fear has no place in me. I will not listen to the enemy's lies. I believe Your Word of truth and power for my life. I know goodness and mercy will follow me all the days of my life. Thank You, God!

Encounter 24

Cast Your Cares

CAST YOUR CARES. You may be thinking, "How is that possible? Do you have any idea what I'm going through or what has happened to me?" No, I may not know your specific situation, but there is a Father God Who does. With His unconditional love and support, you have the potential to overcome every trial and temptation.

God's promise to you is:

> *For surely goodness and mercy shall follow me all the*
> *days of my life,*
> *and I will dwell in the house of the Lord forever.*
> (Ps. 23:6)

The key is to realize that every situation we may have to go through will pass. David wrote in Psalm 23,

> *Even though I go through the valley of the shadow of*
> *death, I will fear no evil, for You are with me,*
> *Your rod and Your staff will comfort me.*

David realized that he wasn't going to have to stop in the valley—he was going through the valley. This is the way it is for us as well. We are going through our trials, and with God's protection and comfort, we will have His peace and victory.

What area do you need comfort in right now in your life?

_____

_____

_____

_____

_____

Are you willing to let it go, and forgive if necessary, so you can move through your valley?

_____

_____

_____

_____

_____

Let's not surrender territory to the enemy that does not belong to him. Let's trust what we read in the Word. Let's cast *all* our cares upon the Lord and ask Jesus to sustain us. Let's internalize the knowledge of who we really are as God's child and be willing to walk in the victory He has planned for us.

Prayer: Thank You, Father, for loving me. Thank You that despite my storm and my shortcomings, I can trust You. This too shall pass, and I take authority over every fear. I cast every care on You because You know what's best. I refuse to take this back on. Thank You that I can trust You to bring me out of every bondage. In You alone, I am free and walking in victory! Amen!

Encounter 25

Achieve What You Believe!

IN THE BOOK OF PROVERBS, we find wisdom for every area of our lives. In Chapter 18, verse 21 it says, *"Words kill; words give life; they're either poison or fruit—you choose."*

Can it really be that simple? I can choose, and I can be accountable for what I say? Imagine if you recorded all that you say during any given day. Later, when you replayed the recording, what would it sound like to you? Would you approve, or would you wince and shrink back from what you heard?

Have you ever said something and then asked yourself, "Why did I just say that?"

_____

_____

_____

_____

_____

When you searched deep within your heart, were you utterly convicted by what you just said? Did you ask yourself: "Where did that come from?"

_____

_____

_____

_____

_____

Are you willing to be intentional with your words? Thinking before responding or reacting?

_____

_____

_____

_____

_____

The power of our words can change our course for good or for bad.

If you're not happy with certain aspects of your life, including your walk with the Lord, it's likely caused by your own internal belief system. But the good news is that you can reshape your beliefs, alter your actions, and develop positive results. However, it first starts with a willingness to do so! Are you willing?

Prayer: Father, please forgive me for any stubbornness in not believing that Your ways and thoughts are higher than mine. This means I don't always have to understand or even like my circumstances, but I can trust You to deliver me from every adversity because You love me. I *will* take authority over my thoughts, so they line up with Your Word. I will spend time in Your Word, trusting the Holy Spirit to renew my mind to Your way of thinking. Your Word says, "As a man thinks in his heart, so is he ... out of the abundance of the heart the mouth speaks." I will trust Christ to put a guard over my words, so they bring life to me and all those around me. Thank You, Lord.

Encounter 26

Reflections

RECENTLY, MY HUSBAND read a book that discussed in great detail the words we say to ourselves and how those words represent our thoughts and personal beliefs. He learned that our actions are almost always consistent with those thoughts and beliefs, and all our behaviors are automatically driven by our subconscious minds. In other words, *we often behave, without consciously choosing, in accordance with how we believe.* Knowing this, wouldn't you think it would be of paramount importance to believe in things that are true about ourselves as opposed to that which is untrue?

That book has had a *huge* impact on us. It caused our family to look inward, to dissect our words, and determine what we truly believe about ourselves, about God, and anything else.

> Whatever the mind of man can conceive and believe, it can achieve. —Napoleon Hill

This is why it is so important for us to take the time to truly reflect upon our thoughts.

Why do we beat ourselves up when we don't do things exactly like we think they should be done?

_____

_____

_____

Do you call yourself unflattering names?

_____

_____

_____

Have you ever beat yourself up for not spending time with the Lord or not reading the Word on a daily basis? Did it result in feelings of guilt and shame?

_____

_____

_____

The enemy loves to stir up these negative emotions of not "being enough" in all of us. However, these negative thoughts keep us from getting closer to the only One Who can change us.

Prayer: Thank You, Lord, that I "have the mind of Christ." I know this means I can think right thoughts, which will produce the right beliefs to propel me into the great plan and purpose You have for my life. Thank You that in You I am victorious in my thoughts and beliefs. I will take the time to reflect upon Your ways and Word for my life so my words will line up with Your words. Amen!

Encounter 27

Submit Your Thoughts

ARE YOU WILLING to search your heart, beliefs and values? Will you allow the Holy Spirit to help you carefully choose your words from now on? Will you then focus on what you hope will achieve your intended outcome? For example, ask yourself the question, "Am I in my emotional brain (reacting) or thinking brain (responding)? When we stay in our emotional brain, we are basing our experience on how we are feeling at that current moment. Our feelings are constantly changing and evolving, like the clouds in the sky. However, when you make the choice to use your thinking brain, holding fast to His promises, then you can respond based on His truths and promises.

Submit your thoughts and words to Our King, Our Lord, Who has the ultimate plan for your life! Trust in Him, for He is Sovereign and *Wise*, and He *loves you*! Do you truly believe He loves you? He *chose* you! He *died* for you! Should there be any question?

In Isaiah 35:4, the Word encourages us, *"Tell everyone who is discouraged to be strong and don't be afraid! God is coming to your rescue!"*

Can you think of a time you worked yourself up with thoughts about something that never happened?

_____

_____

_____

What caused you to think that way in the first place?

_____

_____

_____

What could you have done differently to change the outcome?

_____

_____

_____

I encourage you to take some quiet time and really think about what you are saying to yourself. If it's not uplifting, reframe your thoughts. Submit your negative thoughts to the Lord and seek Him for truth. This will begin a new pattern of how you believe, therefore, how you think, feel, and act. This process will take some time and practice, but once you start to submit your old ways of thinking and doing things, you will see a distinct positive change. The way to succeed is to be consistent and practice daily. Ask the Lord to do this through you. The Word says, *"Take control of what I say, O LORD, and guard my lips"* (Ps. 141:3 NLT).

Prayer: Thank You, Lord, for changing my beliefs and thought life so I can be aware and intentional with what I say. I need You, Lord, every second to guide me and give me wisdom. I am willing to submit my thinking to You because I believe and trust that You will burn out *all* that is not of You! When I quote Your Word, I know that I can expect great things to happen and see positive changes, in Jesus' Name. Amen!

Encounter 28

A Paradigm Shift

A PARADIGM SHIFT is a fundamental change in approach or underlying assumptions. What causes us to assume anything? It's our thoughts ... what we perceive to be the truth. We all have assumed things before and ended up in a not-so-good place. This is why it's key to stay connected to the Holy Spirit to lead us and guide us. He is the Spirit of Truth, so He knows how to keep us on the right track ... in every area.

> *He who has an ear, let him hear what the Spirit says*
> *... To the one who is victorious. I will grant the right*
> *to eat of the tree of life in the paradise of God.*
> (Rev. 2:7 NASB)

Have you ever experienced a paradigm shift? Did your perception differ from reality? If so, did you respond (thinking brain) or react (emotional brain)?

_____

_____

_____

Are you willing to focus on Jesus and wait for His answer?

_____

_____

_____

Are you willing to be content in this unsettled world? Will you push out the distractions that infect your being and rob you of joy, rest, and purpose?

_____

_____

_____

When we can make these changes and do and think His way, we have created a paradigm shift. The Apostle Paul spoke about this in Philippians 4:11–13,

> *Not that I speak from want, for I have learned to be content in whatever circumstance I am ... in any and every circumstance I have learned the secret of being filled ... I can do ALL through Christ who strengthens me.*

You may wonder how this can be accomplished. Are you willing to lean into the discomfort of your feelings and not react to your emotional brain? Instead, respond with your thinking brain by feeding and drinking His Word, trusting in the Holy Spirit to renew your mind. Trusting in Him and resting in His truth will affect change in your thinking.

Prayer: Thank You, Lord, that Your Word is truth and life. When I quote it, faith arises, and I know that I can do all things through You because Your Word promises that You will strengthen me in every area of my life. I praise You Lord for Your unconditional love and plan for me. Amen.

Encounter 29

Pleasure or Purpose

WE ALL HAVE STORIES we can tell about our lives and the experiences we've had. Some are good, and some have been not so good. As you reflect on these times, do you understand what caused the outcome? Was the root cause always a reaction or action based on your thinking? We know the Word says, *"As a man thinks in his heart, so is he"* (Prov. 23:7).

Ask yourself, "What was I thinking?" Were your overall thoughts because you desired pleasure, satisfaction, and joy? Were your thoughts directed toward a more purposeful outcome?

These questions will lead us to recognize how we think, believe, and behave on a daily basis. Pleasure is instant; however, is pleasure always the best? In fact, when led by our impulses (emotional brain), often shame and guilt invade our souls and leave us to focus on self, leaving us sad and empty. This sadness can come in like a flood and overwhelm our system, burying us in our feelings.

Have you ever made a quick decision for instant fun and instantly knew it was a mistake?

_____

_____

_____

Was your self-talk negative feedback followed by guilt and shame?

_____

_____

_____

Negative self-talk can become a habit that becomes difficult to break. Shame and guilt have big mouths, and they can talk loudly. What or whose voice are you listening to—the culture or God?

_____

_____

_____

The culture tells us we need it right now! No need to wait! Our brains are flooded with multiple messages on how we should look, behave, and live. When we invite our flesh in, pleasure takes over. However, the Bible teaches us to be _disciplined, self -controlled, and prepared._ When we live for purpose, which comes from the Holy Spirit's direction, we have a deep sense of complete satisfaction, inner peace!

Prayer: Father, help me today to be willing to follow Your leading in every area of my life. Help me understand that there is both pleasure and fun in following You. You created me to experience every good and perfect thing in You. Thank You for loving me and choosing the best plan for my life. The joy of the Lord is my strength. Thank You!

Encounter 30

Honor and Wisdom

THE BIBLE TELLS US throughout the Book of Ecclesiastes that Solomon had much, yet he considered it all to be a folly. He searched for a deeper meaning in life beyond what he could see. As a result of his quest, God honored him—and he was known as the wisest man. Even though his path was not easy, He chose to recognize that God is ALL powerful. Solomon set his mind and thoughts on what was eternal. He realized that this world was fading away and robbing him of his ultimate purpose—Jesus!

This book can be summed up in this verse.

> The end of the matter; all has been heard. Fear God and keep his commandments, for this is the whole duty of man. For God will bring every deed into judgment, with every secret thing, whether good or evil. (Eccl. 12:13–14)

Job was another man who experienced both good and bad during his walk with God. Job 36:11 tells us, "If they obey and serve him, they will spend the rest of their days in prosperity and their years in contentment."

In the New Testament, the Apostle Paul, who also knew both plenty and hardships, says:

> And He has said to me, "My grace is sufficient for you, for power is perfected in weakness" .... Therefore, I am

well content with weakness, with insults, with distress, with persecutions, with difficulties, For Christ's sake, for when I am weak, then I am strong. (2 Cor. 12:9–10)

The promises in these Scriptures remind me that earthly pleasure is short term, but His satisfaction can and will fill my deepest appetite and leave me content.

What are you chasing? Fame? Success? Pleasure?

_____

_____

_____

Are you willing to change and discipline yourself in His word, truth, and ways?

_____

_____

_____

Prayer: Thank You that I can choose to change. I submit myself to Your ways. I want my life to reflect stability, so I'll walk securely in *You*! I am grateful for my new heart that desires to repent, and seek You. Amen.

Part Two

Identifying Emotions

Encounter 31

Removing Fear

WE ALL HAVE EXPECTATIONS of what our lives should look like, what we will or will not accomplish in life, what kinds of relationships we will or will not have, and even how our lives should appear to others—our family, friends, and coworkers. We all have these expectations of ourselves, others, and even of God.

What happens, though, when things take a turn for the worse? Suddenly, without warning, a storm appears on the horizon, and dark clouds close in on your heart? Whether it is literally the weather attacking your home or a phone call with disappointing, negative news, your first reaction is the same. Fear grips your entire being, and you desperately lash out to try to control everything around you in a vain effort to protect yourself or those you love.

Can you relate to feeling this way? Have powerful, fearful, negative emotions attacked and overwhelmed you?

_____

_____

_____

How did you cope with this? Did you run and hide in fear?

_____

_____

_____

Did you want to blame someone—yourself, others, God? Where/whom did you go to for answers?

_____

_____

_____

When these things happen to us, it is not a pleasant time. Fear means business, and when it shows up and tries to attach itself to you, it can paralyze you. However, we know that to change anything, action is needed. But how? What action can remove this kind of intense fear?"

The first action is to know that God always has a plan and call on the Name of the Lord. We don't ask, "Why, Lord," or "How did this happen to me?" Instead, we ask, "What do you want me to do through me now?" Whether you brought the trouble on yourself or someone else did, God still loves you. That's why His plan for you has not changed. Use your faith, which eliminates fear. Ask Him to help you. He has all your answers.

Prayer: Father, help me to trust You. Fear has no place in my life, and I will not be afraid of my circumstances. I know my footsteps are ordered by You, and I will follow You so I can have a joyful, fulfilling life. Thank You for loving me and for the plan You have for my life. In Jesus' wonderful Name we pray, Amen!

Encounter 32

Negative Feelings

JOHN PIPER, THE BAPTIST PASTOR, founder, and leader of de-siringGod.org, and the chancellor of Bethlehem College and Seminary, writes, "It is utterly crucial that in our darkness we affirm the wise, strong hand of God to hold us, even when we have no strength to hold him."

Maybe you have lived through such a dark time in your life when it seemed things were completely out of control. You even wondered, "Will I be able to get out of bed today?"

Have you ever had trouble getting out of bed because of your circumstances?

_____

_____

_____

_____

_____

Has sin crept in—through your choices or others—to add more fear and doubt to your purpose?

_____

_____

_____

_____

_____

When darkness tries to overshadow everything in your life, who or what do you draw upon for help? Where do you find your source of strength?

_____

_____

_____

_____

_____

At times like this, there is only One Who can ever help us—Who can turn things around. It takes faith and trust in our God (Who is Spirit). When weariness overtakes you and your mind is flooded with overwhelming negative thoughts like anger or sadness, you must center yourself in Jesus, your Savior, Deliverer, Strong Tower, Refuge, and Strength. He loves you, and He has an awesome plan for your life. When we believe this, we can have joy in the midst of our greatest struggle—joy that is based upon our personal relationship with Him, joy that casts down every negative emotion. How? Joy is the fruit of the Holy Spirit alive in you.

Prayer: Father, we thank You for Your love and mercy. Forgive me for not trusting You when things around me don't look good. Help me keep my eyes upon You, which brings _life_ to my soul (mind, will, and emotions) and body. Your love produces feelings of joy, not heaviness. I cast all my cares on You, for You will use all things for my good, according to Your Word and plan. Amen.

Encounter 33

Feeling Confident

THE BIBLE SAYS that we can trust in the Lord. We can be totally confident in His love, in His good plan for our lives, in His saving grace, in His mercy and kindness. He is not finished with us yet. This is not the way it will always be—nor the way you will live from now on.

As we learn to follow Him and rest from our own thoughts, we will experience His goodness. The Word says,

> ... all the while to work and to will His good pleasure in your life. (Phil. 2:13)

Trust Him to work all things out for your good, He will do it. He has promised, and His promises are true!

Can you hear and then obey His voice, despite how hard or painful it may seem at the time?

_____

_____

_____

_____

_____

Can you give thanks in all things, knowing that He will help you in every situation?

_____

_____

_____

_____

If you've ever been hurt by someone close to you, it may seem hard to trust again. However, you won't find anyone more faithful to His Word than the Lord. If He says it, He will do it. In fact, the Word says in Isaiah 55:10-12,

> *For as the rain and the snow come down from*
> *heaven, and do not return there without watering*
> *the earth and making it bear and sprout, and*
> *furnishing seed to the sower and bread to the eater;*
> *So will My word be which goes forth from My*
> *mouth; It will not return to Me empty, without*
> *accomplishing what I desire, and without*
> *succeeding in the matter for which I sent it.*
> *For you will go out with joy and be led forth with*
> *peace; The mountains and the hills will break forth*
> *into shouts of joy before you, and all the trees of*
> *the field will clap their hands.*

Prayer: Father, my heart desperately wants to believe and trust in Your goodness. I give You my dreams, false expectations, and the lies that I believed for a season. Forgive me. Help me to trust in You and receive Your peace, joy, and love in exchange for the enemy's lies. Thank You for loving me and having a plan for my life. I accept it, and I will follow You. Amen.

Encounter 34

Anger

EPHESIANS 4:26, 27 STATES,

> *In anger do not sin. Do not let the sun go down while you are still angry, and do not give the devil a foothold.*

This is God's Word to you and me. In Robert D. Jones' book, *Uprooting Anger,* he defines anger as "a universal problem, prevalent in every culture, experienced by every generation." So, what exactly is anger, and what causes it to have such a stronghold in our lives that it literally can be passed down from generation to generation?

Most of the time, when feelings of anger aren't dealt with, they deepen into bitterness and unforgiveness. Both cause the body negative side effects like physical and mental illness. The root cause of anger comes when things happen to us that we can't control—good or bad. These circumstances cause us to have emotions that we don't know what to do with.

Have you ever just exploded over something and later thought, "Where did that come from?" Have you ever lost control of your emotions?

_____

_____

_____

_____

_____

Did you eliminate those emotions so they wouldn't bother you again?

_____

_____

_____

_____

_____

When we don't take the time to examine the origin of negative emotions, we end up burying them within, hoping to hide or ignore them. However, when we do this, the emotions not only deepen within us, but they are transferred and passed down to our children. Today is the day to make the decision, "No more!" We will not carry these feelings into tomorrow.

Prayer: Lord, help me to recognize the root of my emotions. I don't want to bury them any longer. Reveal to me the real issue, so I can submit it to You for deliverance and healing. Thank You that You came for me to be healed in every area physically and emotionally. I receive Your work on the cross and believe I am made totally whole in You. Praise You, Lord.

Encounter 35

Victim Mentality

MANY TIMES, we are quick to blame others and are unwilling to take responsibility for our own thoughts and actions. We may even try to blame God for our shortcomings and play the role of the victim. For some, this seems to be a healthy way to cope with the circumstances. This allows us to blame our shortcomings on someone else, which becomes their problem—not ours!

This appears to be a workable solution, as long as nothing happens to bring those feelings back up. We're good, right?

We all know this doesn't really solve the problem. So how do we clean out our heart so that anger, jealousy, abuse, and rejection cannot remain? It's first important to ask the Lord. He has the answers.

Why am I bitter toward You, others, or myself?

_____

_____

_____

Do I have unmet expectations or maybe a false sense of control?

_____

_____

_____

Do I lash out at others in rage with my words?

_____

_____

_____

Does fear play a role in my becoming angry?

_____

_____

_____

If you're willing to ask yourself these hard questions, you will get answers. However, you must let go of past hurts, offenses, and wounds. You *can* live at peace in this troublesome world. Oswald Chambers writes, "Let the past rest, but let it rest in the sweet embrace of Christ."

The Word says, "You're not a victim; you're victorious."

Prayer: Lord, help me to remember that I *am* victorious in You and the great plan You have for me. I can forgive all those who have hurt me because You have forgiven me. Let Your love flow through me, not only to heal my past wounds but to be Your example. Your Word says, I am above and not beneath. I accept that and live a life filled with victory.

Encounter 36

Stinking Thinking

WORLDLINESS IS ALL AROUND US. So how do we cleanse ourselves from lustful and evil thoughts that try to penetrate and manifest in ways that take us further away from the presence of the Lord? We must manage our thought life. The Word says in Philippians 4:8,

> *Finally, believers, whatever is true, whatever is honorable and worthy of respect, whatever is right and confirmed by God's word, whatever is pure and wholesome, whatever is lovely and brings peace, whatever is admirable and of good repute; if there is any excellence, if there is anything worthy of praise, think continually on these things [center your mind on them, and implant them in your heart].* (AMP)

How are we supposed to keep our thoughts holy, noble, lovely, and pure as the Word directs us when everywhere you look, something can cause us to think what we shouldn't? In addition, if we fall into temptation, it's not only guilt that comes, but feelings of anger all over again.

When was the last time you found yourself in this kind of situation? What was the result?

_____

_____

_____

_____

_____

Are you willing to be honest with yourself about what you are thinking?

_____

_____

_____

_____

_____

The ability to think clearly only comes when we are abiding in Christ, which renews our minds. As He lives through us, we become aware *and* can be careful about what we say when things upset us. Living from the Spirit produces self-control. Remember, the power of life and death is in the tongue, and many times our mouths only make the problem even worse. However, the Word clearly states, *"We can do all things through Christ Who strengthens us"* (Phil. 4:13). You can do this!

Prayer: Father, I thank You that Your Son paid the price so I could be free. You can direct my thoughts if I let You, and I choose today to let You have complete authority over every area of my life. You have a great plan for me, and I don't want to hinder that plan by anything I may think or say that would not glorify You. I will complete my race in holiness and purity. Amen!

Encounter 37

Control

WHEN WE CAN'T CONTROL everything in our lives, how do we keep the balance we need to keep moving forward? First, we must be willing to resist our fleshly ways by submitting to the Lordship of Jesus. It is important to humble ourselves before Him—trusting that His promises are true. Then we must resist the temptation. When we do these things, the Bible assures us that evil will flee from us.

> *Submit yourselves, then, to God.* **Resist** *the* **devil,** *and* **he** *will* **flee from** *you.* (Jas. 4:7 NIV)

This requires action on our part.

Are you willing to give up control and submit to the Most High God?

_____

_____

_____

1 Peter 2:11 tells us to *"abstain from sinful desires that war against your soul."* You may ask, "How do I abstain from sinful desires?" First, I must be willing to look inward, being honest with what is going on with me internally. Second, I must be willing to be held accountable. Third, I need support found in a community. Part of this means that I must daily be honest with what I am thinking and believing and

consider whether I react or respond to others out of love. Sometimes, this is a hard test for all of us, especially when we're in the heat of the moment. Ultimately, this also means, I don't always have to have it my way.

What seems to be your "button" that people push, causing you to lose control/respond unlovingly?

_____

_____

_____

_____

_____

Let's learn to start recognizing the things that cause us to lose control and create more negative emotions that have many bad side effects. We need to behave as though our thought life has been renewed through daily reading of His Word. Then we have a plumb line to guide us, and our feelings won't take us down the broad road that usually leads us to destruction.

Prayer: Lord, God, we need You to help us. Let this fleshly side of us yield to Your will and the need to always be in control. I want You to be in charge so I can follow You on the narrow road to having complete victory in every area of my life. This victory is not too difficult for You—I'm willing. Thank You for loving me and creating a great plan just for me. Amen.

Encounter 38

Bitterness

WHEN LIFE THROWS US unfair situations, it's hard to remain calm, let alone positive. Yet during these times, we really see what lies inside of us. It becomes a test of our character. Will we lose control and speak unkindly or will we walk in love? Will we stand strong or react out of fear? Will we become angry and respond out of rage or hold our tongue and say nothing?

The truth is, more times than not, we respond out of habit. We become angry, and even if we don't respond, it's not like we go on our merry way.

Can you think of a time, even recently, when you lost it?

_____

_____

_____

_____

_____

How would you handle it differently? What should you have done?

_____

_____

_____

_____

_____

Do you have underlying feelings of bitterness, anger, or fear?

_____

_____

_____

Usually, whenever we respond to something negatively, the cause is hidden anger, fear, or other negative emotions. This response is an automatic reaction, and the result or direction it takes us in is not positive. When we become angry or upset, it is important to head off those angry responses before they become roots of bitterness that defile our hearts and the lives of those around us. We must allow the Lord to shift our reactions/responses of anger, bitterness, wrath, and rage to thoughts of love and compassion. Is this easy? *No*, it's not, but we can change.

Prayer: Lord, thank You for staying with me. Even when I don't act right, You are still there. I want to repent of any thoughts that are not pure and lovely. Please forgive me and help me submit to You any thinking that doesn't line itself up with Your Word. I will cast down every vain imagination and put You back in charge of my life. Bitterness, you have no place in my thinking or my heart. Be gone, now, in Jesus' Name. Lord, I receive Your peace and walk in victory. Thank You!

Encounter 39

Issues of the Heart

THE BIBLE INSTRUCTS US in James 4:8 to

draw near to God, and He will draw near to you.

This means we must be willing to spend time with Him and bring every negative issue of the heart to Him. He wants us to express our feelings to Him in prayer.

It's important that you share with the Lord what causes you to become unforgiving, bitter, and angry. The Lord can and will heal these broken places deep within you. I learned when I daily allowed myself to draw near to Him, He was able to uproot deeply held, false beliefs and replace them with the truth of His love, forgiveness, mercy, and grace.

Are you willing to spend time with God consistently?

_____

_____

_____

_____

_____

Will you let Him replace your hidden negative emotions with His love and power?

_____

_____

_____

_____

_____

_____

_____

_____

_____

_____

Getting to know someone intimately requires time and energy. Many of us fail in this area because of our busy and hectic schedules. However, when we don't make the time, we are only hurting ourselves—not only in the short term but in the long run as well. God never designed us to do this alone. We need Him to reveal our pure heart to us.

Prayer: Thank You, Lord, for Your lovingkindness and mercy toward me. Please forgive my negative thinking and ways. I repent of every false or negative thought, anger, bitterness, and impure desire. I am grateful that You fill me with Your love that conquers all and brings me peace beyond all that I could think or imagine. I will draw close to You. Thank You that you are closer than my next breath. Amen.

Encounter 40

Worry and Anxiety

How many times a day do you either worry, have anxiety, or seem to be overrun by fear? When these thoughts or emotions rise up, what is your first plan of action? Do you even have a plan?

We know each day can provide an opportunity for all of the above. Therefore, we must decide who sits on the throne of our heart? Who or what controls your thoughts and emotions? Are you going to allow your feelings to override your faith?

What is your first thought when these types of negative emotions arise?

_____

_____

_____

_____

_____

Does it cause you to feel sick to your stomach, or give you other adverse physical symptoms?

_____

_____

_____

_____

It has been medically proven that these types of negative thoughts cause physical illnesses like exhaustion, stomach aches, headaches, and insomnia. The Word tells us in Matthew 6:34,

> *Therefore, **do not worry about** tomorrow, for **tomorrow** will worry about itself. Each day has enough trouble of its own.* (NIV)

Worry and anxiety are both forms of fear. When your thoughts begin to turn this way with all the "What if?" questions, you need to stop what you are doing and ask yourself,

"What am I really afraid of?"

The Holy Spirit will reveal the truth to you, and you will be able to submit all of your fear(s). He is in control—in charge—and His Word declares, "He didn't give us a spirit of fear, but of power, love and a sound mind" (2 Tim. 1:7). This means fear has no place within you! Receive His truth for you today and live free and healthy!

Prayer: Father, I thank You for Your Word. It declares the truth and fulfills Your purpose in all things because it doesn't come back void. Fear has no place in my heart or thinking. I'm free and delivered of any worry and anxiety because my hope and trust are in You, the faithful God. Thank You for loving me and protecting me, even from my own thoughts. I praise You, Lord God. Amen!

Encounter 41

Jesus' Establishment

I LEARNED EARLY in life that fear, worry, and anxiety can derail your purpose. I was plagued with an eating disorder and lived in fear of losing control for many years. The real issue was I didn't let Jesus rule my life.

As a result, the pattern of habitual and evil thoughts initiated destructive actions and behaviors that affected not only others' lives, but my own life as well. When we believe that we can do it by ourselves, we are deceived. Many kinds of addictions require the aid of others, including professional help. However, even with those sources, you will discover there are still those alone times, which make it difficult to overcome all by yourself.

Have you ever felt so alone that you didn't think you could cope?

_____

_____

_____

_____

_____

Have you ever been afraid or doubted whether God would fulfill a promise to you?

_____

_____

_____

_____

_____

What did you do to get rid of the fear and believe Him?

_____

_____

_____

_____

_____

When I finally realized I had locked myself inside this prison, the cause was fear, not faith. Faith is knowing, believing that God will do all that He's promised. Then it's the ability to act upon that belief. As I have journeyed with the Lord, He's been faithful to burn out my fleshly desires. I learned to meditate on the Word, and now I know (believe) God is faithful to His Word.

Prayer: Thank You, Lord, that I can trust You. The Word declares that You are not a man that You should lie, so I know when You say it, You mean it. I will not be afraid. I will not let worry or anxiety have a place in my heart. I will trust You to always direct my path in peace. I will think on those things that bring me joy and hope in You. I will let You rule, Jesus, because my hope is in You. With You by my side, I cannot fail. I am victorious in You in every area of my life. Thank You. Amen!

Encounter 42

Choose Life

WE ALL COME FROM different backgrounds, cultures, social and economic positions, beliefs, religious afflictions, values, and morals—all of which are based on how and where we were raised. This is called our family of origin. Google defines family of origin this way: "the significant caretakers and siblings that a person grows up with or the first social group a person belongs to—often a person's biological or adoptive family."

I'm sure you can tell stories about how you were raised. We all can and do. You might hear your friends say, "I'm never going to make the same mistakes my mom or dad made." Yet, many times, they live out these very same patterns in their own lives. Why? It's because certain habits, reactions, and mistakes get passed down from generation to generation. Some are good, and some are not so good. Some can even be categorized as *curses*.

Deuteronomy 30:19 states,

> *I call heaven and earth to witness against you today,*
> *that I have set before you life and death, the blessing*
> *and the curse. So choose life in order that you may live,*
> *you and your descendants.*

According to this, it's our choice. So if things aren't going so well for us, who is really to blame? However, even if the past circumstances weren't so good—today is a new day.

We can choose life! We can forget the former things and move forward, knowing that God's plan hasn't changed for us.

Do you believe God has the same promises for you, regardless of your history?

_____

_____

_____

_____

_____

When troubles knock at your door, do you use God's promises (faith) for your well-being?

_____

_____

_____

_____

_____

Prayer: Lord, I believe I am secure in knowing that I am a new creation You; the old man has passed away. I am new, free of any past lies of the generations that would try to hold me back or keep me from fulfilling all that You have prepared for me. Thank You for loving me and delivering me. I'm ready to walk by faith, believing all the promises You have planned for me. Amen.

Encounter 43

Focus on the Future

PSALM 103:2–4 TELLS US how David handled wrong thoughts and wrong training. Anytime he was under pressure, David learned to encourage Himself with the promises of God. David learned the way to get out of your past was to stay focused on the future. He encouraged himself with God's plan to provide for him every day and to redeem him from the devil's power.

> *If then you have been raised with Christ, seek those things that are above, where Christ is, seated at the right hand of God. Set your minds on things that are above, not on things that are on earth. For you have died, and your life is hidden with Christ in God.* (Col. 3:3 ESV)

This means we have a brand-new beginning. We are not tied to the things of this world—good or bad. I've heard people tell stories about when their parents got their first phones in their house. It was usually a party-line, which meant you could have up to five others using the same line for calls. Were these first phones this good? Yes, because it gave people a way to communicate with others without leaving their homes. Think about how far we have come today with the networks available to us through cellular phones. Is it good? I think most would agree it's good.

This is the progression we can receive when we learn to do things God's way, trusting His ways to be higher than ours and following His plan by faith for a bright and prosperous tomorrow in every area. Choosing life!

Is there an area you need to trust God in to reach your future destination?

_____

_____

_____

What keeps you from trusting Him? Fear? Doubt? Control? Past experiences?

_____

_____

_____

Your future with God is bright. Keep your eyes on Him. He won't disappoint you.

Prayer: Thank You, Lord, that Your "Yes is yes and Amen." I will keep my eyes on You. "Show me Your ways, Oh, Lord," is what King David prayed, and I ask the same thing. I want to follow You so I can continue to move forward and upward to be closer to You. I want to seek those things that are above and keep my mind focused on things that are above, too, in Jesus' Name, Amen.

Encounter 44

Free from Doubt

HAVE YOU EVER doubted God? I have. I was sorry to admit that my faith wasn't strong enough for the situation I was dealing with, but I knew I had to fix it. So, I made the choice to become still and completely honest with both God and myself. When I did that, He revealed through His Word and prayer why I had doubts—or a lack of faith.

I had put fear and control over my faith. The war that raged within me was from the tension between my spirit and my flesh. It was all rooted in my thoughts, desires, and belief system. I held the false belief that God could not be trusted with my life, my future. Fear and control had become false idols in my heart. My part was to do what it says in 2 Corinthians 10:5,

> *Destroy every proud obstacle that keeps people from knowing God. We capture their rebellious thoughts and teach them to obey Christ.* (NLT)

Do you have idols in the place where God should reign?

_____

_____

_____

Has fear kept you from believing God will do what His Word says He will do?

_____

_____

_____

_____

_____

Have you replaced your doubt with believing Jesus, the Living Word?

_____

_____

_____

_____

Faith is the only solution to keeping us moving forward. Today, I focus on sharing my faith with others. Daily, I work on my thought life, surrendering it to the Lord and His perfect ways. I desperately want and need His freedom over any fear, anxiety, worry, and doubt that prevents me from fully experiencing His love, mercy, and grace. Let us all yield our hearts to Him and become sensitive to the Holy Spirit, rejoicing and being thankful for *all* things, for He is Lord!

Prayer: Father God, thank You that I am free! I trust You and take You at Your Word, for You are faithful and true. Now there is no room for fear because I focus on Your face in faith. I choose to relinquish control and make the choice to trust You. Help me to keep my eyes upon You and cast down anything that tries to be an idol or replace You in my life, in Jesus' Name. Amen.

Encounter 45

Negative Emotions

OVER THE YEARS, as I have journeyed with the Lord, He has been faithful to burn out so many of my fleshly desires. As I meditated on the Bible, He showed me Bible characters who also struggled with fear and anxiety. Sarah, Abraham's wife, was afraid that God could not fulfill His promise that she would have a son in her old age. Yet she had a son because God is faithful to His Word.

> For whatever was written in former days was written for our instruction that through endurance and through encouragement of the scriptures we might have hope. (Rom. 15:4 ESV)

Sarah received her promise in God's time and His way. She had to trust the Lord God, and He delivered on His promise. Reigning Grace Counseling Center's definition of faith is "the knowledge of God's character, the belief that He's able to do all that He's promised, and the trust to follow Him wherever he leads." We know the Word says faith pleases God, and faith without works is dead. This means we must be willing to step out sometimes in faith before we will see the result. However, the result in following Him is always a victory for us!

Are you willing to seek the Lord with your thoughts, desires, and actions—replacing all fears with faith?

_____

_____

_____

Do you have a heart's desire to replace those negative emotions with His truth and allow love to pervade your being?

_____

_____

_____

We must make the choice to become doers of His Word, resting our thoughts, desires, and beliefs in Him. He must be King over our hearts! Every day now, I intentionally commune with Him through prayer and worship. I put Him first. I receive his grace for the day. I have learned it's so much better, even easier, because I yield my heart to Him and I've become sensitive to the Holy Spirit's leading.

Prayer: Father, I need You every second of the day to help me replace negative thoughts that have kept me bound in fear—not in faith. Thank You for replacing them with Your goodness and grace. Lord, Your holy nature is kind and gentle. Remind me of the joy of my salvation! Lead me to a heart that is fulfilled with worship, praise, and thanksgiving! Thank You, Lord. Amen.

Encounter 46

Wounds

GENERATIONAL PATTERNS AND BEHAVIORS play a significant role in how we view ourselves, how we view God, and how we will view others. Our sense of belonging and identity normally comes from our development as children within our families. From them, we learn who we are as individuals. Unfortunately, some have experienced traumas and hardships from a young age that have left significant wounds. Many times, even though these emotions were created years ago, they still cause some to believe the lie that they are unworthy, unvalued, unaccepted, and unloved. As a result, unconsciously (or even consciously), they reject themselves.

When external circumstances pierce one's very soul, the wounds become part of their emotional make-up. A wounded heart can then grow numb and hardened against the world, God, and individuals closest to them. Of course, there are many types of wounds. Some cause people to lash out, have a negative reaction, when triggered by something said or by an unpleasant event.

When we perceive a threat, at that moment, it becomes our reality. We go into a *flight, fight, or freeze* mode in order to protect the very core of our being, our heart, from being crushed one more time. This is a method of coping that seems to lessen the pain from our wounds. We don't want to admit that we are reacting, yet our reactions—even our facial expressions—tell the true story. We are wounded individuals in need of healing.

Have you ever reacted to something and later wondered why it had that effect on you?

_____

_____

_____

_____

_____

Do you have a habit of overreacting because of feeling un-loved or unwanted in your past?

_____

_____

_____

_____

_____

Prayer: Father, please heal me from these wounds and any tormenting lies from the enemy. I know You have made me valuable. You love me—I'm Your child. I believe and trust that Your Word will heal and restore not only me but my entire family. Thank You for my continued victory and free-dom. You are a great and mighty God. With You, all things are possible for my life. Thank You; I receive them, for my good and Your glory! Amen.

Encounter 47

Inner Pain

IF YOU HAVE BATTLED with any kind of deep, inner emotional pain, whether from past experiences, traumas, rejection, bullying, sibling rivalry, parental abandonment, or verbal or physical abuse, then there is no better freedom and help than the Lord Jesus Christ. Isaiah 53:3, 5 describes how these very emotions, negative and unpleasant, were felt by our Lord.

> *He is despised and rejected by men, A Man of sorrows and acquainted with grief ... But He was wounded for our transgressions, He was bruised for our iniquities; The chastisement for our peace was upon Him, And by His stripes we are healed.*

At times, it may seem easier to just shove the pain down inside of us rather than bring it to the light. But it is so worth it to receive His full healing. As we begin this process, we must allow ourselves to be vulnerable, open, and real about our essential need to receive healing—our true identity— who we are as defined by Him (The Great I Am, our loving God, and Savior!). His healing then extends to delivering us from patterns of addiction, abuse, insecurity, unworthiness, pornography, co-dependency, unforgiveness, anger, rage, and any other negative, self-destructive habits we may have. The above verse lets us know He understands and He can heal us.

Take inventory—what past patterns have been repeated from previous generations in your family?

_____

_____

_____

_____

_____

If you're serious about receiving your healing and freedom, what plan of action will you take?

_____

_____

_____

_____

_____

You can be healed of these inner pains and the unhealthy emotions from your past by surrendering lies to Him. He will bring them to truth and strengthen you for this battle—just let Him!

Prayer: Father, help me be intentional in taking action. Please intervene in my life to begin the healing process. Let me feel Your love strengthen me as I let go of every hurt and painful thought. Give me a fresh start that only You can bring—newness of life, peace, security, and unconditional love. I know You know how I feel because You suffered greatly for me. Thank You, Lord. I am fully aware that Your victory is now my victory in every area. The past no longer has a hold on me. Glory to God! Amen.

Encounter 48

Family Beliefs

GENERATIONAL FAMILY BELIEFS play a significant role in how we view ourselves, how we view God, and how we will view others. Our sense of belonging and identity normally comes from our development as children within our own families. From them, we learn who we are as individuals. Unfortunately, though, some have battled with significant wounds from their youth that have caused them to believe the lie that they are unworthy, unvalued, unaccepted, and unloved.

Even in the best of home environments, these feelings of not understanding who you are, or what you're supposed to do or be, keep rising within each one's soul. If you don't know who you are, how will you ever fulfill your purpose? Who gives us our worth anyway?

King David was abandoned by his family, but he still knew his worth. Even while he was watching the sheep, not valued by his brothers or his father, God saw him and called him out so that the prophet Samuel could anoint him to be the next King. In Psalm 103:2–4, we see,

> Let all that I am praise the Lord; may I never forget
>   the good things he does for me.
> He forgives all my sins and heals all my diseases.
> He redeems me from death and crowns me with love
>   and tender mercies.

What a wonderful promise God gave to us through David. This not only encouraged him then but does the same for us today. God's plan provided for him all the days of his life and redeemed him from the devil's power. The promises are still for us today.

Do you believe this to be true for yourself? For your family?

_____

_____

_____

Do you struggle with identity issues—value, worth, etc.?

_____

_____

_____

_____

_____

Prayer: Father, only You can fulfill us with Your love and acceptance. You said in Your Word that even if father and mother reject us, You will not. You will never leave us nor forsake us. Thank You for loving me and making me Your child. I *am* a child of the *King*! I *am* worthy, and I *am* valued. Glory be to God! I am a joint-heir with Jesus Christ, Your firstborn Son. Amen.

Encounter 49

A Hard Heart

WHEN OUR PAST CIRCUMSTANCES are unpleasant, maybe even abusive in certain areas, both physically and verbally, the enemy lies to us. The Bible says, "He is the father of lies." In these situations, the purpose of the lie is to make you feel responsible in some way, and if you are responsible, then what kind of person would you be? Because of this, many individuals, unconsciously (or even consciously) turn on themselves. These external circumstances pierce their very souls and become part of their emotional make-up.

Then the thoughts in the soul (the mind, will, and emotions) cause a greater reaction in one's heart. A wounded heart can then become numb and hardened against the world, God, and the individuals closest to them.

Have you felt that the horrible things that happened to you were your fault?

_____

_____

_____

_____

_____

Did you react in a vain attempt to protect your heart, or did it harden your heart?

_____

_____

_____

_____

_____

At some point, we all have had an opportunity to feel unloved, unwanted, and deeply wounded.

Thank God, Jesus is our healer. Psalm 103:3 says, *"He continues to forgive all your sins, he continues to heal all your diseases ..."* (ISV). He knows how we feel and will help us in every kind of situation, even if we have made poor decisions (sinned) and caused our own injuries. He will still heal us and deliver us to receive freedom and live a victorious life.

Prayer: Thank You, Jesus, for what You did for us on the cross. I can have complete faith and confidence that I am free and delivered of any past emotional baggage. I forgive my offenders just as You have forgiven me. Thank You. I receive Your help to deliver wholeness to my soul and body, in Jesus' Name. Amen!

Encounter 50

Rejection

MANY types of wounds come from different sources. Some cause people to lash out when triggered by something said or by an unpleasant event. What triggers this negative reaction? For most, it is the thought of being rejected. Have you ever felt rejected?

I know I have, countless times. We need more than simply an ability to effectively cope with being rejected. All we really need or want is to belong, to feel loved, and be loved unconditionally.

My friend, there is hope! There is an answer! And this answer is found in our Savior—Jesus. If rejection is part of your story, try to recall who or what rejected you and how it first happened. Then realize that Jesus knows and understands rejection. It says in Isaiah 53:3-5 that He was wounded and rejected by many people. Jesus carried our sins and our emotional/physical wounds to the cross with Him so we could be free and receive His unconditional love. This is what brings us total healing. I know this might sound trite, possibly even like a cliché, but it's true!

What do you want to be healed of right now? Rejection? Abandonment? Inner wounds?

_____

_____

_____

_____

_____

Did you know that Jesus already paid for you to be healed?
It belongs to you. Are you going to receive it?

_____

_____

_____

_____

The enemy, and sometimes even "religion," tries to
make us think we must do something to earn this wonderful, *free* gift from God. Jesus not only paid for our sins, but
He restored us back to a right relationship with the Father.
We can have wholeness in every area of our lives, just like it
was originally in the Garden with Adam and Eve.

Prayer: Heavenly Father, I need You to reveal in my heart
where and when the rejection came in and how it has
wounded me. I believe and trust that Jesus, Who became the
living Word, can heal and restore me. You are good, and
what Jesus did paid it all! I make the choice to run to You. I
receive the work You so desperately want to do in me.
Amen.

Encounter 51

Deep Healing(s)

DURING THE HEALING PROCESS, any painfully deep, inner wounds can appear to be a threat to us as they are being exposed and brought to light. But it is so worth it to receive the complete and full healing. There is also a tremendous benefit for future generations in our family line because we can stop the negative follow-through once and for all. Many times, when someone has been mistreated, it's because their parents were abused or didn't have good relationships with their family members, either. Thus, these generational defects are passed down. Besides, you can't give what you don't have, and many times they just didn't know how to be a good father or mother or do things any differently.

As we begin the process of this deep healing, we must allow ourselves to become vulnerable, open, and real about our essential need to receive healing, belong, and be truly loved. As we make this choice to receive healing from our loving Lord, the result is that we can pass on a different pattern to our children – our identity and who we are as defined by Him (The Great I Am, our loving God and Savior!). His healing then extends to the outward manifestations of being wounded internally—healing us from patterns of addiction, abuse, insecurity, unworthiness, pornography, co-dependency, unforgiveness, anger, and rage.

Let's take inventory: What past patterns have been repeated for many generations in your family?

_____

_____

_____

_____

_____

What have you done to try to correct or change these patterns?

_____

_____

_____

_____

_____

For lasting, permanent changes, we must be intentional in taking action and ask God to intervene in our lives. We do this by asking Him to exchange the lie for the truth. This begins the healing process by breaking old patterns. We must stand in faith, fully expecting His love to enfold us. Only He can bring a fresh start—newness of life, peace, security, and love.

Prayer: Father, I thank You for Your presence in my life. If my earthly parents failed me, You will never fail me or let me down. I forgive them and myself. I am a new creature in Christ, and I *am* Your child. Thank you for the power to break any stronghold the devil has had over my life. I forgive my past generations up to the third and fourth generation just like Daniel asked. Nothing from the past will ever be a weapon against me again. Your love surrounds me like a shield, and I'm so grateful. Amen.

Encounter 52

Shame

IF YOU HAVE EVER experienced shame, you know what a depressing feeling it is. What exactly is shame? Merriam Webster defines it as "a painful emotion caused by consciousness of guilt, shortcoming, or impropriety; a condition of humiliating disgrace or disrepute; something that brings censure or reproach also; something to be regretted." Words and emotions associated with shame are discredit, disesteem, disgrace, dishonor, disrepute, reproach, cheapen, degrade, demean, humble, humiliate, lower, sink, or take down. Now we understand why a spirit of depression hangs on shame.

Many times, guilt is associated with shame because it's what we're guilty of doing that brings on those feelings of shame afterward. Guilt is based on a feeling that something has gone against your morals and values system. Guilt says, *"I have done something wrong,"* while shame is *"the fierce and intense feeling of not being worthy."* The more people experience this intense feeling of unworthiness, the greater they believe they are not accepted and don't have any value as a person. Based on past experiences, we have come to believe that we are not worthy of connection and in some way have failed ourselves, God, and others.

The root word of shame means *to cover*. Do you run and hide as Adam and Eve did in the Garden?

_____

_____

_____
_____
_____

Did depression or other negative emotions come upon you as well?

_____
_____
_____
_____
_____

It's only natural that we would try to cover ourselves. We are embarrassed and feel humiliated. Are we afraid others would find us unworthy of their love or friendship if they really knew us? Maybe we try to defend ourselves and lash out. Either way, the Word says, *"So now there is no condemnation (guilt or shame) for those who belong to Christ Jesus"* (Rom. 8:1 NLT). This means we need to confess our sin and repent. God forgives us. Now, forgive yourself. Cast down those feelings when they come into your mind by quoting this verse.

Prayer: Father, thank You for forgiving me the moment I repent. You cast it from You as far as the east is from the west, remembering it no more. I am forgiven, free of shame forever, in Jesus' Name. Hallelujah! Amen!

Encounter 53

Comparison

THERE ARE TWO MAIN AREAS the devil tries to use to get us to believe his lies and fall into his traps. The first one is the blame game. If we can blame someone, even God, then we have removed ourselves from the role God intended for us to live as victors, because now we have allowed ourselves to become victims. The second trap is comparing ourselves to others. We are uniquely and wonderfully made. If each fingerprint is different, then why would other things remain the same? It wouldn't. The other interesting thing about comparison is that regardless of how many appear to be above you, there are just as many below you.

Bob Goff, author of the New York Times Best-Selling book, *Love Does*, gives us his answer: "We will not be distracted by comparison if we are captivated by purpose." So, let's look to the best-selling book of all time—The Bible, God's Word.

> *Not that we dare to classify or compare ourselves with some of those who are commending themselves. But when they measure themselves by one another and compare themselves with one another, they are without understanding.* (2 Cor. 10:12 ESV)

Theodore Roosevelt said, "Comparison is the thief of joy." Do you want joy—real joy? Then purpose to cease from comparing yourself to others.

In what area of your life, does the enemy tempt you to compare yourself to others? How does this make you feel? In your body? In your mind?

_____

_____

_____

_____

_____

Does it ever make you feel better about yourself, especially if it's honoring you?

_____

_____

_____

_____

_____

It's important that we don't hold or think of ourselves higher or lower than others. The one thing we all do have in common is *we all need the help of a Savior, Jesus Christ*!

Prayer: Lord, we are so grateful that You loved us enough to die for our sins. We are victorious, and despite our actions, we are righteous because we are in You. Thank You for forgiving me once for all. I receive that! You are so good and loving, and I want to demonstrate that same love to others. Amen.

Encounter 54

Guilt

UNTIL RECENTLY, when I was backed into a corner, I have fought, and fought hard. Unfortunately, I have hurt many with my words. When this fierce emotion of guilt came over me, I wanted to attack and defend myself. Unfortunately, this need to protect and guard my heart never ended well. In fact, my relationship with those that I truly love and admire became fragmented because of my actions. The result was I felt even more guilt and even more unworthy of the other person's love.

Consider this passage in Hebrews 4:12–13:

> *For the Word of God is alive and active, sharper than any double-edged sword, it penetrates even to dividing soul and spirit, joints and marrow; it judges the thoughts attitudes of the heart. Nothing in all creation is hidden from God's sight. Everything is uncovered and laid bare before the eyes of him to whom we must give account (NIV)*

God sees us; He understands us, and He has the solution to both guilt and shame. It is found in receiving His love! Instead of trying to protect ourselves or defend our position, what if we changed our narrative, pressed pause, hit mute, took a step back, and became still? What if we allowed the Lord to speak to us words of acceptance and value? The truth is, we are loved and secure in our relationship with Hm.

Do you still battle emotions of guilt or shame? Have you re-pented?

_____

_____

_____

_____

_____

Do you believe "you" can take control of your thinking, or do others "make" you feel a certain way?

_____

_____

_____

_____

_____

I have recently and intentionally chosen to live free and full, to allow myself to become vulnerable and authentic, to be purposeful in my relationships, and then to rest in the knowledge that I belong! Now I choose to take the time to be still before Him and hold fast to His promises.

Prayer: Father, You call me *worthy!* By Your grace, You've *made me* worthy. You know my name. Help me to see that even in my imperfections You are making me whole! I receive Your love and acceptance, and I thank You that I belong to You. I don't belong to this world. Help me when negative feelings override my emotional state. I will choose to focus on You and what You've done for me!

Encounter 55

Snares

The fear of man brings a snare, but he who trusts in the Lord will be exalted" (Prov. 29:25)

THINK ABOUT THE WORD *SNARE*. It's a word that connotes an evil trap. When we think about a snare, we think it's something someone else does. It certainly can be, but according to this verse, we ourselves have the ability to set up the trap with our own thinking. The Hebrew Dictionary defines a snare as "something that lures a man away from his real purpose and then destroys him."

Have you ever been pulled away, distracted slowly from your purpose or calling in life? Have you ever followed after what people say, or what our culture says, instead of God's thoughts and His ways? We all have, and we all still do at times. But why do we fall for the same snare or trap?

What would you say is or has been a snare in your life?

_____
_____
_____
_____
_____

What did you do or are you doing to prevent this from causing you to stumble another time?

_____
_____
_____
_____
_____

Who are you looking to for guidance and freedom? Why?

_____
_____
_____
_____
_____

There is only One Who can and will deliver us and keep us from falling and failing ourselves, others, and, ultimately, our relationship with God. It isn't for us to consider what the world thinks or accepts because we know that even if we are in this world, we are not of this world (John 17:14). We will no longer be ruled by man or his thoughts of us, but of the Lord, our God.

Prayer: Father, we are so thankful that You established the end from the beginning. I purpose to not let myself, or anyone else set, up snares/traps that can deceive me or cause me to stumble after things that are not of You. My eyes are on You. My desires are wholly submitted to You. Thank You for guarding me and protecting me from the trap of the enemy. I know Your Word says he is already defeated and under my feet. I am victorious in You. I will stay close to You and Your wisdom, in Jesus' Name. Amen.

Encounter 56

Desires of the Heart

IN 2012, MY FAMILY made a decision to adopt a little girl we would call Anna. We thought we heard from the Lord and even had confirmation. Later, I realized it was more my idea than my husband's. But even so, wasn't this pursuit noble, good, and honorable? Unfortunately, before I knew it, I was caught up in my own desires that took me further and further from my purpose. I became totally distracted by this idol that had taken the place of my King. This entangled us—not only emotionally, but financially. We were even defrauded by an adoption agency who promised us a healthy baby girl, even though there was no baby intended for our family.

Praying for this little girl dominated my thoughts, and truthfully, I became obsessed with expecting God to move heaven and earth on my behalf. I can now freely admit that I became self-absorbed, self-consumed, selfish and prideful. These disappointments caused me to doubt and question God. Has this ever happened to you? Have you started out pursuing something good but then became disillusioned by the process? Have you become afraid of what others would think more than what God thinks? I sure did.

Have your desires ever become idols and taken up all your thinking/planning time?

_____

_____

_____

_____

_____

When did you realize the truth?

_____

_____

_____

_____

When we begin to follow our desires down this path, it can be deceptive, seductive, and eventually destructive. We may feel like it is *OK,* but I challenge you to ask yourself, "What or Who do I worship?" If your answer isn't the Lord, then check your heart. This is when disappointment and failure try to destroy who we are and our God-given purpose in life.

Prayer: Lord, I give thanks and praise You for Your promises of deliverance. Thank You for already hearing my inner prayer to be set free. Search my heart and test my mind. I want to enter into Your throne room and *completely surrender to You!* As I seek You, show me any idols in my life that are keeping me from hearing *You!* Today, I choose to head in Your direction, not mine! I will not fear mankind, but I will *fear You,* which leads to restoration, freedom, and eternal life! Amen!

Encounter 57

Letting Go

HAVE YOU EVER WORSHIPPED an idol—something other than God? Have you ever chased after anyone or anything that took you away from His presence? At times, we need to ask ourselves these kinds of challenging questions. We need to cause an awakening within us to see the truth.

Unfortunately, at one point I was holding on to something so tightly I couldn't even see the truth. But God intervened in a way I never expected. I was involved in a scary, but injury-free car accident. He got my attention! Both my time and my plans stopped. Later, I headed to church, and my pastor said, "Someone here has a calling from the Lord, but they are running from it."

Immediately tears flooded my face. My husband looked at me and spoke tenderly, "Honey, you are holding on so tightly that you can't even see the road in front of you. Let go!"

At once, my heart became fertile, and I received that word from my pastor and husband. It was actually a word from the Holy Spirit directed right toward my heart. I was instantly convicted and saw this idol for what it was. I repented for what had completely blinded me to God's will for my family.

Where are you headed—toward God or your own idols or desires?

_____

_____

_____
_____
_____

Has there ever been a time you were deceived and followed your own plan, instead of God's?

_____
_____
_____
_____
_____

Trust me, we all have, but that's when we must be willing to repent of our blindness and get back to our real calling and purpose, which is solely to honor and glorify God with *all* of our hearts! Yes, I repented of what had kept me from my Great King. Are you willing to do the same? Open your heart to receive His truth, mercy, and grace.

Prayer: I give thanks and praise You, Father, for Your promises of wholeness and blessings. Thank You for already hearing my prayer to not only be set free but hear the truth. Thank You, Holy Spirit, for leading me and guiding me in all truth. I know You are the Spirit of truth, and I need You in my life. I surrender my thoughts and ways to Your thoughts and ways because the Word assures me that Your ways are higher than mine. I accept that You know me better than I know myself, so You will bring me the desires of my heart that line up with Your Word and plan for my life. Thank You, God. Amen.

Encounter 58

Blind Thinking

WHEN WE BECOME TRAPPED, we are blinded to the truth and deaf to the Holy Spirit's voice. We then try to justify ourselves, and in the deception, we think the snare/idol is a good thing. We even try to rationalize it by thinking, *"I really do not do this too much."* However, these thoughts slowly invade our soul, and we are destroyed.

Snares, idols, or inner desires can be seductive and deceptive. They patiently whisper in our ears and invade our thoughts. They call to us, and looming in the darkness, they wait for an opportunity to entrap us. The evil one comes and attacks the character of God right before our very eyes. He comes at us with lies, and plants thoughts of doubt, despair, and hopelessness until we become overwhelmed — even cornered. He has us penned in so much that we lose sight of the Lord and His promise of deliverance.

But then we read in the Word,

> *If the Lord had not been on our side when people attacked us,*
> *they would have swallowed us alive when their anger flared against us;*
> *the flood would have engulfed us, the torrent would have swept over us,*
> *the raging waters would have swept us away.*
> *Praise be to The Lord, who has not let us be torn by their teeth.*

We have escaped like a bird from the fowler's snare;
the snare has been broken, and we have escaped.
Our help is in the name of the Lord, the Maker of
heaven and earth. (Ps. 124)

Have you ever felt trapped or cornered by the enemy? Did you even realize it was the enemy?

_____

_____

_____

_____

_____

What had you so blinded that you didn't even see his attack coming?

_____

_____

_____

_____

_____

Thank God His nature is kind, loving, merciful, and powerful to lead us to repentance from worshiping anything *but* Him. He wants our whole hearts. Through His truth and grace, He floods us with His unconditional love, forgiveness, and restoration. Hallelujah!

Prayer: Lord, open the eyes of my heart. Remove anything in my life that keeps me from You. Convict my heart, Holy Spirit. I repent and confess every evil thing. I place my life on Your altar. Purge me. Cleanse my motives. I desire to have Your thoughts, beliefs, and desires from now on. Amen.

Encounter 59

Boldness

THE WORD SAYS we are to be bold as lions.

"The wicked flee when no one is pursuing,
But the righteous are bold as a lion."
(Prov. 28:1 NASB)

How is it possible to stay, remain, and live boldly when it looks like everything is crashing in all around us? There is only one way. We must begin by setting a new pattern of living, and it must be done consistently. Just as we get up, eat, and sleep every day, we must focus on Truth—Jesus. He enables us stay in the battle, be obedient, and to trust God in and through every circumstance! He never leaves us, so why would we want to leave Him out of our daily routine.

There are some key steps to take to implement this daily process. Let's look at these.

First, you must be willing to immerse yourself in His Word. Mediate on it day and night.

Now you might be asking, "How can I meditate on it day and night when I work, have kids, etc." As you read the Word, different Scriptures will minister to you. Write them down, memorize them, and meditate on them. Then when things occur during the day, these verses will come to mind. Speak them boldly, declaring your authority in Christ. This is what strengthens us, keeps our faith active, and moves the hand of God.

Second, Seek Him and Only think thoughts that honor and glorify His Great Name. Replace any negative thoughts with positive ones.

Again, this will happen as you learn more of the Word. When fear-filled, doubting, negative thoughts start to come, *immediately* ask yourself, "Is this what the Word says?" Then replace those thoughts with what the Word says. Speak the Word boldly, declaring your victory.

This pattern will take time. How do you see yourself achieving/implementing it on a daily basis?

_____

_____

_____

_____

_____

_____

_____

Just remember, *"You can do all things through Christ, Who strengthens you"* (Phil. 4:13).

Prayer: Father, I thank You for the plan You have for my life. Jesus taught us to pray for daily bread, and I know He wasn't just talking about food. He was talking about our daily "supply" for everything—physical, financial, relational, etc. Thank You that You care about us daily and provide for us the same way. I will read and meditate on Your Word, confessing it daily, placing my faith in You! In Jesus' Name, Amen!

Encounter 60

Courage

THE WORD READS:

> *There is none like you, O Lord, you are great, and great is your name in might.*
> *Who would not fear you, O King of the nations? Indeed, it is your due!*
> *For among all the wise men of the nations and in all their kingdoms, there is none like you.* (Jer. 10:6–7)

When we realize and accept that we are joint heirs of the *King of the nations*, why would we be afraid? His name is the name above all names, so why would we hesitate to use it or be embarrassed to use it, even in public?

Most of us let sin or our imperfect ways keep us from accepting our true and rightful position as a child of God—the Creator of the universe! The enemy loves to tell us we aren't worthy, we can't do that, we will never be good enough. The amazing thing about the enemy's lies is there is usually a wee bit of truth in them. Because of sin, we aren't and never would have been good enough. This is why Jesus came to earth, to be crucified and die, so we could be restored to our original position with God—the perfect position of righteousness that Adam and Eve had when God first created them in the Garden. Through Christ's blood sacrifice, we are now *made* holy. We didn't do it—He *did it for us*!

Our part now is to receive it and walk boldly and courageously in His power and might. If you need some guiding, follow the steps below.

Allow Him to search your heart and test your thoughts daily. Ask the Lord to remove anything that honors, feeds, or builds up the flesh. Then submit those things to Him.

Repent of anything that does not bring Him honor and glory. Quickly, receive His forgiveness, giving no foothold to the enemies' lies.

When we come to Him, repenting and receiving forgiveness, we will be free and able to walk with courage and boldness in Him—knowing that the Holy Spirit's power lives and reigns in and through us, which is far greater than that of the world.

Do you believe that you are called and chosen? Will you walk in boldness and courage?

_____

_____

_____

_____

Prayer: Thank You, Father. I receive Your forgiveness so I can walk boldly and courageously. I love You and thank You for loving me. Apart from You is a life of destruction. I desire a life that sets me apart from the world. Let all things become new in my life, as I purpose to worship You only forever. Amen!

Part Three

Victoriously Overcoming

Encounter 61

God's Strength

ONE SATURDAY MORNING, my family headed toward Roan Mountain State Park, at 5,200 feet elevation, right between North Carolina and the Tennessee line for a hike. We got out of our car and started our trek. At the first rest stop, we took a family photo and decided to keep going. Before long, *everything changed*—the wind drastically increased the higher we went, and the path was muddy, narrow, and steep. Now, the kids began to complain, "Let's stop ... this is too hard ... let's go back!" My husband, Chris, and I tried to encourage them. We told them to press on, keep going, it would be worth it! However, the challenge was almost overwhelming.

Have you ever been in so deep you wondered if you would survive? Are you there now?

_____

_____

_____

_____

_____

What does it take in the midst of the attack to be victorious?

_____

_____

_____

_____

_____

I'm glad to report my family and I made it to the top. *Wow!* What a magnificent, 360-degree view of the mountain peaks and the valley below. We were in awe that God created all of this for His Glory! When we hiked back down, my middle son looked back up at that mountain and said, "Mom, look at what we climbed!" I admit it was an amazing accomplishment. Thanks be to God!

This is and will be the report of us all if we stand in faith, use God's Word, and declare we are victorious. We, too, will look back at a time in our lives when we said or thought, "Wow, look what God has done in my life and through me." Thanking God in advance is how we receive every good and perfect gift from Him. The Word says to,

> *Give thanks in all things for this is the will of God for you in Christ Jesus.* (1 Thess. 5:18)

This doesn't mean you are giving thanks for the circumstances; you are giving thanks *always*, regardless of the times being hard and trying. God inhabits the praises of His people.

Prayer: Thank You, Lord, You are a faithful God Who hears and sees our needs even before we express them. I will give You thanks always, for You love me and want the best for me in every area of my life. I will achieve all that You have for me and be victorious in every way and in every area of my life, for Your glory. Amen.

Encounter 62

God's Wisdom

THE WORD HAS MUCH to say about wisdom. The world will confuse knowledge with wisdom, but there is a huge difference, according to the Word. Proverbs 15:33 states,

> The fear of the LORD is instruction in **wisdom,** and humility comes before honor.

Psalm 107:43 also says,

> Whoever is **wise**, let him attend to these things;
> let them consider the steadfast love of the LORD.

As you can see from just these two verses, this is not what the world seeks when looking for knowledge. What does a reverential fear and humility have to do with wisdom? So why is His wisdom so important? Because He knows it all—He created it—*and* He knows you, far better than you know yourself because He also created you. He knew you before you were ever born.

When we are willing to submit to His authority, we will overcome any obstacle that tries to stop us. The enemy has no power over us, regardless of what our circumstances are saying. Oh, yes, circumstances talk. They have a voice, and many times the words you'll hear will not be positive. If you've ever been through anything traumatic or chaotic, you know what I mean.

When was the last time your situation told you the outcome would be different from God's Word?

_____

_____

_____

_____

_____

What was your reaction to what you heard? Did you believe it, or did you stand in faith?

_____

_____

_____

_____

_____

Sometimes, our paths are steep, hard, narrow, and crooked, and we feel completely out of control. Yet, God, in His lovingkindness, stretches us so that we depend upon Him and His wisdom more and more. He is faithful to carry and sustain us—when we are weak, He is still strong!

Prayer: Father God, I praise You for the trials that test my being and cause me to experience Your wisdom in a way that I have never done before. Lord, even when I don't understand Your ways, I trust You. Your wisdom is infinite, and Your *love* is perfect. Your *grace* flows and renews my spirit. I give You thanks. Help me to humbly surrender everything to You so my path will be victorious! Amen!

Encounter 63

God's Good Pleasure

ANY TIME WE FIND ourselves in tough situations that require hard decisions, we will be faced with questions. "Do I trust the Lord enough to show me how to manage this situation?" Unfortunately, we must be truthful with ourselves at difficult times. I have learned to be grateful, and I praise Him for the season of challenges and uncertainties we experience. It reminds me that He carried me through to victory in the past and He will carry me to victory now.

Sometimes, it's the Lord Himself Who ordained our test or trial in order to accomplish His will in our lives. As our pastor stated, "Maybe you are in the midst of a miracle." Even though your path is uncertain and difficult, God is always working.

Philippians 2:13 says,

> For it is [not your strength, but it is] God who is effectively at work in you, both to will and to work [that is, strengthening, energizing, and creating in you the longing and the ability to fulfill your purpose] for His good pleasure. (AMP)

Do you find it is difficult to truly trust that His love for you is enough to take care of difficult situations?

_____

_____

_____

_____
_____
_____
_____

Why do you think you still run from Him, instead of submitting to Him in tough times?

_____
_____
_____
_____
_____
_____
_____

His plan for us is spelled out in the above verse: **"to will and to work for His good pleasure"** in our lives. Why would someone spend their time planning for someone's fruitfulness if they didn't love them and have great plans for them? It is His strength, not ours.

Prayer: Father, please help me to trust You. I know You love me, and that should be enough. I know You sent Your Son to pay my debt. I receive the benefits of His sacrifice. I know I will be victorious in all things, for You have said in Your Word that You would strengthen me and even create in me the longing and ability to fulfill Your purpose for my life. This assures me that no weapon or trial the enemy puts in my path will stop me. I will complete all that You have for me in Jesus' Name. Thank You, Lord.

Encounter 64

God's Grace

THE WORD SAYS in 2 Corinthians 12:9,

> *But he said to me, "My grace is sufficient for you, for my power is made perfect in weakness." Therefore, I will boast all the more gladly about my weaknesses, so that Christ's power may rest on me.*

We live by His Grace. We have nothing in and of ourselves, yet we have all things through Him. So we let go of everything that does not belong to us and give it all to Him. Only then can we realize that He has paid it all—our debt has been paid in full. Yes, you are His beloved child! Trust His process to bring you into a more intimate relationship with Him so you may know Him and experience *all* that He is and has for you!

I have heard the true meaning of *grace* is: *God's riches at Christ's expense.* If He would tell someone like the Apostle Paul to trust Him because His grace was sufficient, then we need to learn from that example. No one experienced hardship like the Apostle Paul, and yet he depended upon the Lord and the Holy Spirit's direction for every move He made. He received wisdom through dreams and visions, even those that told him not to go to certain cities when he had planned to travel there the next day. These warnings were an extension of God's grace and mercy because of His love for Paul.

God loves us, just like He did Paul. The Word says He is no respecter of persons (Acts 10:34). It's true that Paul had a big plan to fulfill, but we all have a part to play in the great commission. "Go and make disciples," may mean a trip across the ocean for some and a trip across the street for others. We all can do our part when we rely on His grace for the specifics.

When was the last time you experienced His grace in your life?

_____

_____

_____

_____

_____

Was it a specific word or direction?

_____

_____

_____

_____

_____

Prayer: Father, I thank You for Your grace. When I am weak, You are strong. I receive Your power to complete my purpose for Your Kingdom. In all my ways, may You receive the glory and honor. Amen.

Encounter 65

God's Peace

THE BIBLE SAYS that we can trust in the Lord—being totally confident in His love, His good plan for our lives, His saving grace, His mercy, and His kindness. He is not finished with us. Whether our day-to-day is currently good or bad, it won't always be this way. As we hope in Him, as we abide and rest from our own thoughts, we will experience His hope. Not only will the trials come to an end, but even our good times can become more fulfilling. The key is to truly trust Him to work all things out for our good—He will do it. He has promised, and His promises are true!

God doesn't just promise we will come through, but He promises to manifest His Life as Peace during the problem. In John 14:27, we read,

> *Peace I leave with you. My peace I give to you. I do not give to you as the world gives. Don't let your heart be troubled or fearful.* (CSB)

His peace is a gift to us. Only God can give you this peace. Don't look to the systems of this world for your inner peace. The calm that the Lord brings to us is supernatural—it is beautiful because it is the fruit of the Holy Spirit.

Have you learned it's much easier to go through tough times with the Lord than without Him?

_____

_____

_____

_____

_____

Can you remember a time when you didn't trust God and it didn't turn out so well?

_____

_____

_____

_____

This is when we learn to lean on the Lord because His ways and thoughts are higher than ours. He knows us better than we know ourselves. When we let go and trust Him, peace like a river will flow out of us. We will see His mighty hand move on our behalf. We often become amazed because we experience Him in new ways, ways we could never have arranged or planned for ourselves.

Prayer: Thank You, Lord, for being willing to give me Your peace. Help me learn how to immediately turn to You in any circumstance. Your ways are so much better than mine, and I will trust You to carry me through every situation. Thank You for the great plan You have for me—plans to prosper me and give me hope for a bright and victorious future. Amen!

Encounter 66

God's Rest

Is it possible to rest in this fast-paced society we live in? How does one learn to manage all the emotions and thoughts that fill our hearts and minds on a daily basis? Obviously, this is where we must rely on the Word to comfort us and bring us the peace and rest we so desperately need to endure what lies ahead of us.

The word *peace* in Hebrew is *Shalom*, which means "nothing missing, nothing lacking or broken—total wholeness." We can see why the Lord Jesus said He was giving us His peace, but not the peace the world knows. When we allow ourselves to trust Him, the peace we receive is His "Shalom." This means all is well, even during the middle of the storm.

However, Truth that brings us peace is a choice we must make by focusing on Jesus. Choosing Truth enables us to leave the frustration, the agitation, the worry, and anxiety at the feet of Jesus and trust Him as our Peace.

Jesus said,

> *Come to me, all of you who are weary and burdened,*
> *and I will give you rest"* (Matt. 11:28 CSB)

Are you battling something today that is trying to steal your peace and rest?

_____

_____

_____

_____

_____

What does God's Word say for you to do? Are you following it or your own emotions?

_____

_____

_____

_____

_____

Receiving supernatural peace in the midst of your storm is possible. You *will make it through*! If you are having a hard time sleeping at night, you are letting the enemy lie and tell you that the circumstances are bigger than your God. You know God is bigger than anything you are going through right now. Let go! Let God! When we are so emotionally attached to things, it's hard to hear what the Holy Spirit is telling us to do. But you can hear His voice, and you will find rest if you let yourself rest in Him.

Prayer: Thank You, Lord, that You see my situation and You already have all the answers I will ever need. I will rest in You, lean on You, and trust You to be my every provision. You are so faithful. You have never let me down before, and I know You are working on my behalf right now as well. Glory be to God! You are a mighty God, and nothing is too difficult for You! Amen.

Encounter 67

God Is With Us

DON'T STOP PRAYING, expecting, believing, hoping, and trusting in the Lord. Moses encouraged the Hebrew people many times during their wanderings in the desert on the way to the Promised Land.

> *Do not be afraid. Stand still, and see the salvation of the LORD, which he will work for you today.*
> (Exod. 14:13 NHEB)

Fear is one of the strongest emotions the enemy uses to keep us from moving forward so we won't receive His promises. However, God told us more than 365 times in His Word to not be afraid. We need to believe by faith and stand on the Word. We also need to remember that we are not alone in our trials or daily journey through this life.

The Bible tells us that Jesus is with us at all times. He is alive and present in times of famine, in the midst of your dry, desert land. Yet, through faith in God, He will show Himself strong to those who put their trust in Him. Believe in His goodness, for God is a good God. The devil is the one who came to kill, steal, and destroy. God comes to bring fresh living water to fill your well and give you hope in the midst of your storm. Peace will be your strength when you choose to believe in the goodness of the Lord, despite what the enemy tries to take from you.

What are you waiting on for God to bring victory into your life?

_____

_____

_____

_____

_____

Are you standing on His Word, believing in His goodness, power, and love to make the change?

_____

_____

_____

_____

_____

Prayer: Lord, I choose to give You any and all fear and receive Your peace, trusting that You know my every situation because You are always with me. Forgive me for not talking to You first about things I'm going through. I purpose to rest in You and wait patiently for You to act. I purpose to stand strong and be at peace. I know You will perform Your Word as it pertains to my life, my family, or the circumstances I find myself in right now. I trust You, my Lord, to bring about a great victory for my benefit. Thank You, God! Amen.

Encounter 68

New Beginnings

Isaiah 43:1–3 says,

> *Fear not, for I have redeemed you; I have called you*
> *by name, you are mine.*
> *When you pass through the waters, I will be with*
> *you; and through the rivers,*
> *they shall not overwhelm you; When you walk*
> *through the fire you will not get burned,*
> *and the flame shall not consume you. For I am the*
> *Lord, your God the Holy One of Israel, your*
> *Savior.* (ESV)

What a promise of hope God gives us in this Scripture—a promise that no matter what we are facing today, if we put our trust and hope in Him, we will overcome!

Today, because of His promises, this can be a new beginning for you. It is a paradigm shift from believing you are a *victim* to believing you are a *victor*! This happens when we trust in Him. Whatever your crisis may be, Jesus is the healer of *all* suffering and sorrow.

God reminds us in Isaiah that no matter what, He *is* our Savior. He tells us that we have been redeemed! He knows us personally. He loves us unconditionally and calls us by our name! His desires to walk with us in our darkest valleys and change us from the inside out.

Are you willing to obey and trust Him in the process?

_____
_____
_____
_____
_____

Can you believe there is a new beginning in your future—
you can move from *victim* to *victor*?

_____
_____
_____
_____
_____

The Bible says God's Word is a light unto our feet. There is never a bad time to turn to the Word for guidance, assurance, and comfort. Jesus is the Word made flesh—turning to the Word is like turning to Jesus Himself. He is present. Even holding the Bible close to us can physically make a difference.

Prayer: Father, I choose to lay down every fearful thought that keeps me a victim. I choose the victorious life You planned for me from the very beginning. I choose to trust You. Thank You for healing me and delivering me from the fear of the past and what is to come. You have numbered my days, so I trust You to fulfill Your plans and purposes for my life. Thank You for loving me and for the great plan You have for me by fulfilling Your purpose for my life in Jesus' Name. Amen!

Encounter 69

God's Promises

IN THE OLD TESTAMENT, God gave Abram a new name—Abraham. This name meant "father of many nations." This was quite a challenge for Abraham to believe because he didn't have even one child at the time. In fact, he and his wife were both past childbearing years. But what a promise—to be the patriarch of nations! However, now the question was, *how do you complete what God has called you to do when you're not even physically capable of doing it?*

Unfortunately, in the beginning, Abraham followed his wife's leading instead of God's and tried to complete the work in his own timing and by the work of his own hands. His wife's handmaiden became pregnant and gave birth to Abraham's firstborn, but this wasn't God's plan or His best. Years later, Sarah gave birth to Isaac, who carried on the lineage and blessings to us even today. God is faithful to His promises.

> *Now, therefore, fear the Lord and serve him in sincerity and in faithfulness ... choose this day whom you will serve ... but as for me and my house, we will serve the Lord.* (Josh. 24:14–15)

Will you hold fast to the promises of His Word? Will you choose to believe Him?

_____

_____

_____

Will you stand for God's plan in your family's lives and even for future generations?

_____

_____

_____

Just as Abraham did, I choose to believe in this same promise for my family and our future generations. I purpose to take hold of His promises, press in, and trust in Him for myself and my family's future. I believe Your promise You have given me and my future generations that we receive everything for Life and Godliness in You. I will stand in the gap for future generations to make a difference. Will you do the same?

When Abraham waited and believed God, He saw the plan of God unfold before Him. Abraham traded his old life for a new one, and we can too, through the finished work of Jesus.

Prayer: Father, today I thank You for sending Your Son. Jesus, I thank You for coming to earth to die in my place, bringing me a brand-new life. I ask You to forgive my past generations, and I break every curse in Jesus' Name. I (we) will follow You all the days to come. My family lineage will walk in the blessing and abundance You promised all the family of faith through our forefather, Abraham. Amen.

Encounter 70

Recover It All

TRIALS COME WHEN we least expect them. Suddenly our world is turned upside down. When that happens, what do you do? Where do you turn for hope and healing? Will you believe and hold fast to His Word?

No matter how dark the valley or how deep the pit in which you find yourself, God promises that you *will not* be overwhelmed, consumed, or burned even a little bit by the circumstances. What a powerful promise of comfort, hope, and truth to you and to all those who are hurting, broken, and see no way out of their confusion and troubles.

> *When you go through deep waters, I will be with you.*
> *When you go through rivers of difficulty, you will not drown.*
> *When you walk through the fire of oppression, you will not be burned up; the flames will not consume you.* (Isa. 43:2 NLT)

Like David in the Old Testament, you can "recover it all!" Hallelujah! God provides everything we need—God provides healing for our entire being—the physical, mental, emotional, and spiritual. Healing implies wholeness. He restores our joy as we spend time in His presence. Remember, He never leaves us, nor does He forsake us in times of trouble. We can count on Him. We can be filled with gladness of heart because of His mercy, goodness, and grace, which He pours out to us without measure. Therefore, we rejoice and are at peace as we hope in Him!

When you find yourself in a dark place, what verse are you believing that restores your faith and brings joy?

_____

_____

_____

_____

_____

What is it about this verse that brings you comfort and builds your faith?

_____

_____

_____

_____

_____

God keeps our foundation and trust in the Lord firm and secure. Not only will we overcome, but God restores everything the enemy stole from us.

Prayer: Father, thank You for recovering everything the enemy has tried to steal from me. You are a gracious and loving Father, and the plans You have for me prove that. I will stand strong on Your Word, and I will recover all I've lost because You are faithful to perform Your Word. Amen!

Encounter 71

Sanctification

GOD PROMISES THAT in your darkest night and deepest pit of despair, even when you feel trapped, you will *not* be overtaken by evil. Instead, you'll overcome *all* the work of the enemy. God already has you in position—He has already begun a new work in your life, and He won't stop until you and I are complete in Him. This process is called "sanctification," which is defined as "the act or process of acquiring sanctity, of being made or becoming holy." During this process, God burns out all that is not of Him.

The second part of this definition is profound, as you are being "set apart for a particular use in a special purpose or work; to make you holy or sacred." God is calling you to a higher place—to trust Him in your weakest moments. Clearly, God sets us apart. Why? It's because He has a special and holy purpose for each one of us.

> *Now may the God of peace himself sanctify you completely, and may your whole spirit and soul and body be kept blameless at the coming of our Lord Jesus Christ.* (1 Thess. 5:23 ESV)

Why is this so important in our walk with the Lord? It's what sets us apart from the world. It is our witness to others—our testimony—that in the midst of evil, we are more than conquerors. We are victorious in every situation, regardless of what it looks like or, especially, how we feel.

Are you enduring difficult circumstances right now?

_____

_____

_____

_____

_____

Do you fully realize that this will all work for your benefit so you can praise God for the end?

_____

_____

_____

_____

_____

The Word tells us we are made new creations, the old man has passed away. This means that our dependence on flesh must be surrendered. Some lies that motivate flesh do not give up easily. By standing on His Truth, you can do it!

Prayer: Lord, thank You for what You did on the cross. We will lay down our old ways, so we can be all You created us to be. We will walk in Your victory for our lives so we can run our race victoriously with You by our side. Holy Spirit, thank You for leading me. I ask for Your wisdom, and I receive it now, in Jesus' Name. Amen.

Encounter 72

God Is For You

WHEN WE ENCOUNTER dark valleys, deep pits, uncontrollable circumstances, and trying times leave us exhausted, confused, and weak, we sometimes can't even find the strength to pray. Unfortunately, we may feel this way more often than we would like to admit.

At times, we may even have become angry with God because of the circumstances. You may have even questioned "why" you had to go through such anguish of the soul. We read in 1 John 15:2–6,

> *Every branch in Me that does not bear fruit, He takes away; and every branch that bears fruit, He prunes it so that it may bear more fruit. You are already clean because of the word which I have spoken to you. Abide in Me, and I in you. As the branch cannot bear fruit of itself unless it abides in the vine, so neither can you unless you abide in Me.*

These verses explain that sometimes, in order to bear more fruit, we must be pruned or have some things cut off or cut out of our lives. In the fall, when a gardener cuts his plants back, does the plant scream and holler? Complain? No, but come spring, it bears more and more fruit. God's plan for us is the same.

Have you ever wondered if God has left you in a predicament where you couldn't find your way?

_____

_____

_____

_____

_____

Will you choose to believe that God is in control of your life and is on your side?

_____

_____

_____

_____

_____

God is *for* you, not *against* you! He will lift you up and encourage you, never destroy you. Just stay close to Him. Let the Holy Spirit direct and guide you to your next step. You cannot fail when you let Them lead Your way! You will bear more and more fruit in your life in every area.

Prayer: Lord, I thank You that Your Word says You will cause *good* to come out of this situation. Help me accept this trial as Your work. Help me to understand that You are setting me apart, for a "special purpose or work and to make me holy or sacred." Prepare me for the call You have upon my life. I thank You and praise You. I surrender to Your ways, and I will be stronger because of this. Amen!

Encounter 73

A New Day!

THE LORD PROMISES in His Word that we are His. The key is whether we really believe the Word. The Word says for us to believe who Jesus says He is and who He says we are. When we experience Christ as life, we will desire to consistently stay in His Word, pray, and trust in the promises of the Bible. In this we will see this new season come to pass in our lives. The Power of His Word sharpens our swords.

Revelation 21:5 declares, *"I [Jesus] am making all things new"* (ESV).

However, a new day may require some new patterns of thinking —going in a different direction.

Are you aware of old patterns of thinking that cause you to choose flesh? What are they?

_____

_____

_____

_____

_____

Do your old patterns of thinking line up with scripture? What is the scriptural truth that will enable new patterns of thinking to emerge?

_____

_____

_____

Maybe it is time to lay down some of your fleshly desires that have held you captive. Maybe you have been banging on a door that will not open. Or maybe you have become complacent in your walk with Christ. Regardless, He never leaves you. He is always working on your behalf to get you to your new, ultimate destination.

The great thing about becoming new or being positioned to experience new is just that—it's new! One of the definitions of the word new is "just beginning or beginning anew and regarded as better than what went before." God's new for us is definitely better than what went before. We must be willing to accept and embrace His new, even when we don't understand it or maybe even don't agree with it in the beginning. He knows it all, and He loves us too much not to keep us moving forward in the right and *new* direction.

Prayer: Father, please forgive me for not being willing at times to follow Your leading. I do trust You, and I know You have *new* and better plans for me than I could ever have for myself. Thank You for not giving up on me but staying with me through it all. I embrace my *new* day with You. Show me Your ways. I will follow You always in Jesus' Name. Amen!

Encounter 74

A Hope and a Future

WE DON'T HAVE TO BE concerned or afraid of God's plans for us because He assures us over and over in His Word that He loves us and only wants the best for us. He has a plan. He has always had a plan. When Adam and Eve sinned, God didn't have to turn to the angels and ask in horror, "What should I do now?" The Word says He knows the end from the beginning.

> For I know the plans I have for you," declares the LORD, "plans to prosper you and not to harm you, plans to give you hope and a future. (Jer. 29:11)

Ask yourself this question: "How much better could my life be if I completely immersed myself in Himself and allowed Him to live His life through me—His ways—His plans? What would happen if I listened to Him in how to prepare for the day?

_____

_____

_____

_____

_____

Are you ready for a new and brighter future? What needs to change?

_____

_____

_____

_____

_____

Time is ticking, and seasons are changing. Today is a new day! Will you be intentional in this new season—both internally and externally? God has a wonderful plan for your life! Let's experience all He has for us by allowing Him to live His life through us, as us. Staying in His Word enables us to remain strong, regardless of the circumstances. He is our shield and buckler. During trying times, isn't it comforting to know that He is not only with us, but He goes before us, shielding us and protecting us from the enemy? With Him on our side, how can we lose? We can't! The enemy is under our feet. Maybe that's why the Word says when trouble comes to look up! Our focus doesn't have to be on the circumstances, but on our God—our Deliverer!

Prayer: Father, I pray that we will make the choice today to live in Truth and take responsibility for our actions. Lord, I choose to pray, meditate on Your Word, and worship Your Holy name. Lord, I need You to give me vision, to renew and refresh my soul, so I can mount up with wings like eagles, not be weary, and walk and not faint. Lord, let me run daily with great conviction of our purpose and calling in this new season. Thank You for Your plans—I receive Your great plan and future for my life. I can do all things through You! Hallelujah! Amen!

Encounter 75

God's Sovereignty

ONE DAY I SAT on the beach, so close to the water's edge I could feel the mist hitting my face. It was stinging my cheeks and eyes. I vividly remember and can almost taste the bitter, salty water on my lips. As I sat there, I pondered this verse:

> *And we know that God causes all things to work together for good to those who love God, to those who are called according to His purpose.* (Rom. 8:28 NASB)

Have you ever wondered how God was going to turn your mess around?

_____

_____

_____

Have you ever wondered how God could bring good out of what appears to be devastation or bring calm out of chaos?

_____

_____

_____

What does it mean for you to be called according to His purpose?

_____

_____

_____

Sovereignty is understood to be the full right and power of a governing body to govern itself without any interference from outside sources. It is the ultimate in supreme power and authority. This is why we know God is the *final* authority in *all* things. What He says goes. However, He gives us a choice—free will. We can believe this is true and read and obey His Word, believing and trusting in faith that it will come to pass, as He lives His life through us, or we can disregard it. We can go our own way, doing things as we see fit.

As Dr. Phil used to ask his patients, "How's that working for you?" Their response was, "It's not." Why would we choose another way when the God Who owns it all and created us knows what is best for us? Many times, it is a false sense of pride. We not only think we can't do it, but sometimes we think we don't deserve it. We think we need to clean our act up before we can expect anything from God. Listen, my friend, if we could have cleaned ourselves up, Jesus would not have had to come and die for us. We need Him and the Holy Spirit to show us our gifts and calling and God's great plan for our lives.

Prayer: Father, God of all, thank You for choosing to send Your Son so I could be reconciled back to You and Your great plan for my life. You are sovereign, and I respect and honor You. Lead me in the path I should go. I will choose to submit to You and follow Your ways for my life. Amen!

Encounter 76

God's Character in Us

THE APOSTLE PAUL WROTE in Romans chapter 8 that we can trust God in all things. No matter how it looks at any point, He is always working things out, and in the end, the result will be good. How can that be? How can "all things" work for my good? God's ultimate purpose is to cause us to be conformed to the image of Christ. His goal is to restore each of us as His children to the image of God!

He takes what is damaged, broken, wounded, and even shameful and brings healing, wholeness, peace, and joy. This great work is accomplished in our day-to-day lives as the Lord allows us to experience both happiness and sorrow (just as Jesus did while He lived on the earth), with the result that His own character is formed within us.

Have you experienced His joy in the midst of your trials, suffering, or loss?

_____

_____

_____

_____

_____

Are you willing to let the Lord access your heart—trust Him for strength to receive joy and peace?

_____

_____

_____

_____

_____

What happened that changed your circumstances to become a message of hope and joy?

_____

_____

_____

_____

I have certainly experienced His joy during my trials more than once. When the waves rage and the water is fierce, the day seems cold, and we feel isolated and lonely, we can still experience His joy. Even if our emotions try to overtake us with sadness, this is when we must still our souls, simply knowing and believing that He is God. He knows best. Right now, choose to believe that God is in control. He is *for* us! He is perfect, and He is trustworthy. He is also infinite in His wisdom and perfect in His love for us!

Prayer: Lord, I choose to trust You in every area of my life, in both the good times and the bad, believing Your promises. I trust You to work behind the scenes, using the circumstances for my good because I do love You. Thank You for loving me and bringing me closer to You, Lord God.

Encounter 77

A Present Help

IS YOUR LIFE all messed up and you don't know where to turn? Do you sense confusion all around you, and you are searching for a way out? None of these are pleasant circumstances, but many times, these crisis situations are an opportunity to build your faith in the Lord. If you put your trust in Him, He will deliver you, but He will do it His way, not your way.

God is all-powerful. But you must listen to His voice and not the voice of the devil. You must fight the enemy in the spiritual realm, not in this natural physical realm. As you yield to His Holy Spirit, trust God to deliver you, and resist the enemy, you will gain the victory over your crisis experience.

God is the same yesterday and today, and He will be the same tomorrow, too. He never changes, and He is always right there. The Word says,

> God is our refuge and strength, a very present help in
> trouble.
> (Ps. 46:1)

In the midst of our broken heart and crisis experience, God is there to usher in love, joy, and peace, *if* we will receive it! You need a strategy beforehand that will enable you to gain the victory over these crises. The best one I know of begins with crying out to God and receiving His authority to do battle and win! Matthew 28:18–20 says, *"All authority in heaven and on earth has been given to me; go therefore ... and I will be with you to the end of the age."*

Do you believe this? What would keep you from being obedient?

_____

_____

_____

_____

_____

Will you cry out to God? Believe? Continue to walk and stand in faith until you see completion?

_____

_____

_____

_____

_____

Throughout the Bible, ordinary people cried out to Him in the midst of their brokenness and God offered His hope, peace, joy, love, provision and deliverance. We are all in a spiritual battle, and we must stand with a shield of faith in victory!

Prayer: Father, I will not give up! You are in charge, and I will win every trial by following You. Thank You for being there for me and with me each day. I am more than a conqueror in You. Hallelujah! Amen and amen!

Encounter 78

God-Given Authority

THE BIBLE INSTRUCTS US TO

resist the devil, and he will flee from you! (Jas. 4:7)

But how can we resist his deceptive and cunning ways? First, we must recognize the attack for what it truly is—a lie of the devil. We must use our God-given authority to resist that temptation, snare, or deception and do as Jesus did. We must speak directly to Satan and tell him to get out of the way. Boldly say, "Stop it, devil; that's enough! In the authority of Jesus' Name!"

This may be new to you, as it was for me a while back. But when we learn to call upon God for deliverance, when we speak Jesus' name out loud, the Bible tells us that our enemy will then cease the attack. He must always quit his harassing at the mention of the Name of Jesus!

Have you asked God for help? Have you called on the Name of Jesus and seen immediate results?

_____

_____

_____

_____

_____

If you haven't, why not? Unbelief? Do you know or accept your position as God's child?

_____

_____

_____

_____

_____

In what area of your life do you need to use your God-given authority?

_____

_____

_____

_____

The enemy is the father of lies. Just before Jesus ascended back to Heaven, He said, "I have been given all authority, and now I am giving you all authority." The question is, "Will we receive it, use it, and speak it to receive the victory in our lives?" There is power in the Word and His Name. So, truthfully, we have no right to ever feel powerless in any situation or circumstance.

Prayer: Father God, I take the authority Christ gave me, and I speak to every lie and fleshly desire in my life that does not line up with Your Word. I AM an overcomer. I can do all things through Christ Who strengthens me. I *am* above and not beneath—the head and not the tail. Thank You, Lord Amen.

Encounter 79

The Victory

WE SHOULD ALWAYS EXPECT Christ to be victorious over our circumstances. To receive this is to trust the Lord for the answer—even before the answer arrives. In praising and rejoicing, we recognize that as we pass through life, our trials are only temporary. Jesus, our Savior and Victor, has already paid the price for our deliverance. He promises that He will be with us and that help is on the way even when we cannot feel, hear, or see a way—we must trust that He is *Jehovah Shammah*, *"the Lord Who is right there"* with us! We must persevere and be persistent in our worship, in prayer, and in meditating upon His Word.

The Word also says we are to,

> *Give thanks in all circumstances; for this is the will of God in Christ Jesus for you.* (1 Thess. 5:18 ESV)

Give thanks in all things, for this is God's will. This doesn't mean that the Lord has brought this thing into your life, but regardless, we can still rejoice because He is the One Who can and will change it for our good! His eyes are always upon us. We need to hold fast to His promises! Believing, trusting, obeying, and never giving in or giving up!

Have you seen the Lord do amazing things or turn a situation around?

_____

_____

_____

_____

_____

Was it in your own life, someone else's life, or both?

_____

_____

_____

_____

He is the same yesterday and forever. If He's done it before, then we know and have the confidence that He will do it again, and again, if necessary. Do you believe it?

Prayer: Lord, I thank You for the promises in Your Holy Word. They encourage me to know that You always have both my front and back. Thank You for Your sacrifice on the cross, which gives me all authority over the devil. You know *all* things—even though my crisis may be a surprise to me, You are never surprised. Lord, I praise You for providing an answer for every need I have. Thank You, for giving me the victory over the enemy, every time I need it. You never tire of giving me the victory, for which I praise you, God!

Encounter 80

Stay Awake

WHAT HAPPENS WHEN we only see our circumstances or we lose sight, which makes it hard to engage with His peace, joy, and rest? During the storm, it is hard to maintain our balance. The more you focus on the Truth the more your emotions will line up. By looking unto Jesus, and believing Him, the sooner yours is the victory.

So how do we maintain during a battle? We *need to stay alert!* We need to *wake up!* The seasons of our lives are changing quickly. Souls are perishing, and we, as believers, need to be alert and engaged—prepared every moment.

Revelation 16:15 states clearly,

> *Behold, I am coming like a thief! Blessed is the one who* **stays awake***, keeping his garments on, that he may not go about naked and be seen exposed.*

From this verse, we see that the Bible teaches us to be prepared, engage, and to stay alert—to wake up and become alive. We must become aware of the battle that rages all around us. The question is, "Am I willing to be prepared, alert and engage at all times?" What happens when we get tired and exhausted? We quit or lay down, and then we become vulnerable and easy prey to the enemy. However, what if no matter what, we got up, got dressed, hit our prayer room, and read His Word every day?

Do you have a regularly join Jesus in prayer?

_____

_____

_____

Why do you think it's important to pray and read the Word on a daily basis?

_____

_____

_____

Now, I understand sometimes things come up, and it's not possible to pray, or you cannot even pray. I have been there, but this is your word for today. *Get up! Stay awake*! And keep going! Reach out to someone. Look up! Pray, believing and trusting that He will bring you through.

Prayer: Lord, Your Word is true. It is "yes" and "amen," which means if You said it, You will do it. I will choose to read and pray consistently because I desire to grow and experience a knowing of You. I *am* led by the Spirit, not my flesh. I will be watching, ready to do Your will, Heavenly Father. Amen!

Encounter 81

Stand Firm

I KNOW WE HAVE all faced our share of trials and struggles. Battles come in all shapes and sizes. But what do we do when the battle doesn't cease? Now we have years of this distress under our belts, and the future doesn't look any brighter. Sometimes, the battle may not cease—in fact, it may intensify. So how can we make the shift—not just to cope or survive, but to thrive and be victorious when literally everything around us is under attack?

I have found there are four things that can encourage hope for the outcome.

- Be prepared
- Engage
- Be alert at all times
- *Stand firm!*

The Word says in 1 Corinthians 15:57–58,

> *But thanks be to God! He gives us the victory through our Lord Jesus Christ. Therefore, my dear brothers, stand firm. Let nothing move you. Always give yourselves freely to the work of the Lord, because you know that your labor in the Lord is not in vain.* (NIV)

Will you willingly trust Christ to examine how He wants to use your time and talents throughout the day?

_____

_____

_____

_____

_____

In order to be prepared, what do you already see as something that will try to steal your time?

_____

_____

_____

_____

Jesus tells us (as the Bride of Christ) to wake up those who sleep and arise to our King. Will you be ready? Will you keep your lamp burning? Every day we need to encourage each other to press on, not to run, become isolated, or even quit. He promises us that it will be worth it.

Prayer: Father, open my eyes and mind to be prepared, alert, and engaged in Your *Word*. I repent of anything that keeps me from being focused on You. I know if I will trust you my life, I will be able to stand firm, which is Your command. I refuse to let what I see in the natural move me. My hope and faith are in You. I will not be shaken. I'll stand for You and for Your Kingdom! Amen!

Encounter 82

Weapons to Stand

WE'VE ALREADY ESTABLISHED repeatedly that you will face battles, unfortunately, on a regular basis. However, the key to victory is to know who your enemy is and the weapons to use to obtain your victory. Ephesians 6:12–17 makes it clear who our enemy is and how we fight the good fight of faith.

> *For our struggle is not against flesh and blood, but against the rulers, against the authorities, against the powers of this dark world and against the spiritual forces of evil in the heavenly realms.*
>
> *Therefore, put on the full armor of God, so that when the day of evil comes, you may be able to stand your ground, and **after you have done everything, to stand. Stand firm** then, with the belt of truth buckled around your waist, with the breastplate of righteousness in place, and with your feet fitted with the readiness that comes from the gospel of peace. In addition to all this, take up the shield of faith, with which you can extinguish all the flaming arrows of the evil one. Take the helmet of salvation and the sword of the Spirit, which is the word of God.* (NIV)

God did not leave us here to fight the devil without proper weapons. Are we using what He gave us? Do we even understand the true battle we are fighting? Do we blame others, or do we realize it's the enemy working through them to be a weapon against us?

Think of something or someone the enemy has used to offend you?

_____

_____

_____

Can you see why he would be able to use them? (They have deep emotional hurts/wounds.)

_____

_____

_____

_____

Hurting people hurt people. You can't give what you don't have. So now, when others try to offend you, step back and look at how hurt and beat up they are themselves. This is what helps us to walk in love or even turn the other cheek as Jesus directed us to do. This is the first sign that we should be praying for them even more, as difficult as this is for us.

Prayer: Lord, thank You for teaching me how to use Your weapons, not only to defend myself but to forgive and help others who don't even know they are being used by the enemy. I will continue to stand firm so I will see victory in every area of my life in Jesus' Name. Amen!

Encounter 83

Hope in the Fire

ANY TIME WE FIND ourselves in the heat of the battle, we have to make some decisions. Will we stop, breathe, and remind ourselves of God's Word, or do we believe the lies, twisted with truth? During these times, we come to realize how important it is to have renewed our mind to the Word. It's also important to focus on *hope*, while we're going through the fire.

There are several ways we do this.

We must **accept** that this season in the refining fire is the will of God for our lives. We must receive hope that this season is for our good.

We must **submit** to the process of the refining. (And friend, it is not easy!)

We must **allow** the Lord to stretch our faith so that we can trust Him and His intentions toward us—that they are all good! This really takes faith.

We must **pray** in the spirit, for there is power in prayer to the Most High God. When we press into Him and then run with Him, we will see beneficial changes start to take place.

I call these "Job" moments in life. Remember the biblical story of Job? At the end of his book, Job said,

> *With my ears I heard Thee, but now my eyes see Thee.*
> (Job 42:5)

Obviously, the trials brought Job to another depth in His relationship with the Lord. He could now see Him!

Have the battles you've gone through brought you to feel closer to the Lord?

_____

_____

_____

_____

_____

What have you learned that is truly a valuable life-lesson?

_____

_____

_____

_____

_____

See Him for Who He really is for you and your family. Let your mind be renewed to His truth.

Prayer: Father, I thank You for exposing any lie that has kept me from moving closer to You. I want to see You. Thank you for refining my soul and letting me be found acceptable in Your sight. My hope is in You and Your plan for my life. My eyes will be on You and not these circumstances. Thank You for lifting me. Amen!

Encounter 84

Choose God

I HAVE EXPERIENCED, for more than one season in my life, a time filled with testing and refining. It was necessary for Him to burn out *all* the lies—lies that had been hidden. I had considered them to be the truth, but in fact, they were lies of the enemy. Now it was necessary to make a choice, which I was able to do easily because my deepest desire was to see Him and follow after Him. I chose to move closer to Him. This came one day after I was reading about King David. Regardless of his trials, and he had some, He never gave up on His relationship with God. His psalms prove that repeatedly.

What about you? Will this be your desire and choice too?

The Word reads:

> *You must love the LORD your God with all your heart, all your soul, all your strength, and all your mind. And, Love your neighbor as yourself.*
> (Luke 10:27 NLT)

If we are truly going to receive Jesus as our Peace that God wants for us, we must make this choice. Who will we serve?

Who do you serve—money, family, security, status, recognition, etc.?

_____

_____

_____

_____

_____

Past family issues, childhood concerns, being loved, etc., why are these things so important to you?

_____

_____

_____

_____

Choose today to press into His unconditional love for you and receive *all* that He has for you, just as I did. Allow His transforming power to come into your heart and heal you of past wounds, past rejection, and give you His mind, His thoughts, and His peace. You will move faster and further ahead with Him as Your lead than you could ever do on your own. Choose Him—He has already chosen you.

Prayer: Father, I can't thank You enough for choosing me. I choose to focus on You as first in every area of my life. I can't do this without You, and I don't want to do this without You. Thank You for never leaving me or forsaking me. I know Your ways and thoughts are higher than mine, and I need that in my life. Please forgive me! I will choose You and follow You always, in Jesus' Name. Amen.

Encounter 85

God's Kingdom

GOD HAS BEEN THERE for me in my time of spiritual famine. Jesus made me brand new—completely free—feeling alive! He birthed in me a new beginning and a deep restoration that changed my heart and life forever.

The Word says He is no respecter of persons. This means that what He does for one, He will do for everyone. He can and will do this for you and your family, too, if you ask Him and allow Him to make the necessary changes.

Today, I present before you an opportunity—to make a choice. You can choose to walk in faith or to walk in fear. You can decide to be healed or to continue to live a miserable life. It may sound too easy, but it really can be that simple. The Word says,

As a man thinks in his heart, so is he. (Prov. 23:7)

You can change everything by choosing the Truth which leads to the Lord's will and way. Seek His face. Pray to Him. Ask Him to do what is needed in your life to deliver you from all evil and all of the enemy's lies.

Will you make the decision to change some thinking patterns so you can reach a different outcome?

_____

_____

_____

_____

_____

What is one of the first things you will do differently? Why?

_____

_____

_____

_____

_____

My hope is that you will choose to really start living in God's Kingdom. And what is this Kingdom? It is righteousness, peace, and joy in the Holy Spirit. You can walk in the fruit of Love, Joy, and Peace every day because you live in union with Him. You can think on the Lord. You can set your affection upon Him. You can pray to Him and He will hear and answer you! Daniel prophesied, *"But the saints of the Highest One will receive the kingdom and possess the kingdom forever, for all ages to come"* (Dan. 7:18).

Prayer: Father, thank You for setting up the Kingdom for us to enjoy and prosper in. I will choose You in all my ways. Thank you for making me completely new and giving me Your thoughts. I thank you for choosing me to live *in Your Kingdom* and experiencing righteousness, peace, and joy, and receiving Your mercy and grace from now on. I receive this transformation right now in Jesus' Name! Amen!

Encounter 86

Speak the Word

DID YOU KNOW you can have whatever you say—that life and death are in the power of the tongue?

Proverbs 18:21 says,

> *Words kill; words give life;*
> *they're either poison or fruit— you choose.*

Imagine if you were to record all that you said during any given day. Later, when you replayed the recording, what would it sound like? Would you approve, or would you wince and shrink back from what you heard? At times, I've said things and then thought, "Why did I just say that?" What about you? When you searched deep within your heart, were you utterly convicted by what you had said? Did you ask yourself, "Where did that come from?" The power of our words can change our course for good or for bad.

When was the last time you said something and immediately wished you could take it back?

_____

_____

_____

_____

_____

Did you ask yourself why you said it? What was the under-lying root of the statement?

_____

_____

_____

_____

_____

_____

If there are aspects of your life that you're not happy with, including your walk with the Lord, it's likely caused by what you have been saying, which now has become your own internal belief system. The good news is that by trusting Christ your thoughts, words, and beliefs can be altered. This will change your actions and attitude, *if* you're willing to do so! Again, the choice is yours, *and* you don't have to wait another day to decide to change. Today can be the first of many fruitful days. All you have to do is change your thinking.

Prayer: Father, please put a guard over my mouth. If my words don't line up with Your Word. I want the words of my mouth to be pleasing to Your ears, and the meditations of my heart to be acceptable in Your sight. I trust you to speak positive, faith-filled words that will change my life and uplift those around me, in Jesus' Name. Thank You for all You are doing in my life. To You be all the glory! Amen!

Encounter 87

Right Beliefs

Recently, my husband read a book that discussed in great detail the words we say to ourselves and how those words represent our thoughts and personal beliefs. He learned that our actions are almost always consistent with those thoughts and beliefs, and all our behaviors are automatically driven primarily by our subconscious minds. Napoleon Hill, author of one of the 10 best-selling, self-help books of all time, wrote, "Whatever the mind of man can conceive and believe, it can achieve."

We often behave, without consciously choosing to, in accordance with how we believe. Knowing this, shouldn't it would be of paramount importance to believe in things that are true, especially when those beliefs are about ourselves? Why is it so easy to believe the negative when it comes to our own lives? Why do we even ask ourselves negative questions? An example could be, "Why do I fail at spending time with the Lord? My intention is to seek Him; yet, *daily*, I fail because the kids need this or that, my husband needs me, or I'm just too busy!" Does this sound familiar?

Do you beat yourself up with negative feelings/emotions from doing what you shouldn't or not doing what you should?

_____

_____

_____

_____

_____

How can you change this and eliminate the guilt and shame that follows this line of thinking?

_____

_____

_____

_____

_____

If you were to reframe your question from negative to positive, do you think a paradigm shift would take place? YES! The questions we ask ourselves come from our beliefs, which then shape our actions. Initially, you have a thought, then you speak it as words, then your actions become consistent with those words! If you change your question, then you can reprogram your subconscious mind to redirect your behavior. How do we start the process? First, we change our thinking, and then we speak forth positive truths. From there, we will act accordingly!

Prayer: Lord, I choose with my beliefs and thought life to become aware and intentional of what I say. I need You every second to guide and give me wisdom. Holy Spirit, help me carefully choose my words from now on. I will focus on Your outcome and believe that I will see Your results in every area of my life. I will submit my thoughts to You and live in victory for my good and Your glory, in Jesus' Name. Amen!

Encounter 88

Finding Purpose

HAVE YOU EVER asked yourself, "What is my purpose? What did God create me to do? Do I have a calling?" We all have, *and* I'm happy to add, we all have one. However, many times, our circumstances and some of the not-so-good decisions we have made in our lives tell us otherwise. Maybe you have been bound by an addiction, such as pornography, shopping, or maybe you are solely focused on yourself. Maybe you have been the one who has been offended by your husband, kids, or other family members. No matter what you have experienced or are experiencing, God still has a purpose and a call on your life!

Have your circumstances caused you to believe that your purpose/calling is impossible to achieve?

_____

_____

_____

_____

_____

Ezekiel 34:25–27 tells us,

> *And I will make them and the places all around my hill, a blessing, and I will send down showers in their season; they shall be showers of blessing. And the trees of the field shall yield their fruit, and the earth shall*

yield its increase, and they shall be secure in their land. And they shall know that I am The Lord, when I break the bars of their yoke, and deliver them from the hand of those who enslaved them. (ESV)

We do not get to choose our seasons, nor our circumstances. However, we do get to choose our mindset. We also get to choose how we will spend our time. So now is the time to decide. Will you persevere and fight for things of the Kingdom, or will you become distracted by the world and allow the enemy to take territory that does not belong to him? Filling your mind with head trash only causes you to slip further from God and His plan for your life.

Sometimes, this is not an easy journey. In fact, true perseverance is hard! What helps is when we remind ourselves of the truth in God's Word, such as, *"I can do all things through Christ Who strengthens me ... I have the mind of Christ, so my thinking/beliefs will line up with the Word of God ... No Weapon formed against me shall prosper, and every word spoken against me I can condemn because that is my inheritance."*

Prayer: Father, today I choose to follow, speak, and believe Your Word in faith, which is truth for my life. When I follow You, I will walk out the plan/purpose/calling You have established just for me before the foundation of the world. I cannot fail because the Holy Spirit leads me and guides me into all truth. He is my comforter, and I will be strong in the Lord and the power of His might! Amen.

Encounter 89

Pressing On

IN OCTOBER 2001, my husband, Chris, and I ran the Chicago marathon. It was 26.2 miles! This pressed, pushed, and stretched me further than I could have ever imagined. As we came up on mile 22, I wanted to quit—sit down and stop! My body was weary, my feet hurt, and my legs were so heavy. I was miserable. Now crying, I asked Chris, "Can we please sit down?" My husband, the great encourager, said "*No*! We must keep going, pressing onward. We are almost done!"

I'm glad to report that I did not quit! But what if I had? What if I had simply laid down? Obviously, my ending would have been much different.

Instead, I chose to listen to his voice, which pressed me onward toward the goal. Then, in the last .6 miles, something came over me—something changed internally—something happened physically. Chris and I took off and sprinted full force for the finish line. We crossed it together, lifting our hands up! We held on to each other for strength.

Now you may be thinking, "What does this have to do with me? I can't even make it to the gym down the street, let alone run a marathon." You may be right, but we all have come up against tough times, financial issues, health problems, divorce, or unfaithfulness—things that have made us want to quit. In times like these, we must turn to the Living Word, Jesus, and stand in faith that God still has a plan for us—a great plan—if we don't quit. In times like these, we must *press on*!

Can you think of a time, or are you going through a time, where you would like to call it quits?

_____

_____

_____

_____

_____

Will you take hold of God's promises for you, for your husband, for your family?

_____

_____

_____

_____

At times like these, no matter what, we must persevere, pray, pursue peace, and keep pressing on. God is quick to come to our aid. The Word says to call on Him in times of trouble, and He will heal, deliver, and come to our rescue. Our part is to press on toward the high calling of our Lord.

Prayer: Lord, thank You today for the energy and strength to continue to move forward in You. I can and will do all things through Your strength and power, in Jesus' Name. Thank You for being with me during these times. I know Your Word says, *"This too shall pass!"* Thank You, God! Amen!

Encounter 90

Praise Him

WHEN YOU ARE WEAK, tired, worn out, and completely exhausted by your circumstances or you have endured physical or emotional pain that stretched you beyond what you thought you could accomplish, how do you move forward? When your life seems completely out of control, how do you recover? How do you move from point A to point B? How do you live out your purpose in the midst of your grief, sorrow, and heartache? How does one love and forgive others? Yourself? God?

All of these are powerful questions. In the midst of our greatest trials, we search for the answers, but sometimes they aren't what we want to hear, so the biggest question should be, "What does the Bible have to say about my situation? What does it instruct me to do now?"

More times than not, most of our serious issues deal with being offended. Someone has done us wrong! We know the Word tells us that we need to forgive. This is not easy. When we are hurt, the last thing we feel like doing is to forgive, love, praise and pray. However, when you make these choices, the power of the cross comes *alive*. Something deep within you begins to stir, an ember that wants to burn bright for your husband, family, and, more so, for Christ. When you begin to praise Him, the spirit of heaviness lifts and depression, bitterness, anger, fear, and anxiety begin to fall to the ground.

Have you chosen to praise Him during a troublesome time and experienced His freedom?

_____

_____

_____

_____

_____

If not, are you willing to begin a new way of thinking/recovering emotionally?

_____

_____

_____

_____

I have had many seasons of enduring heartache, betrayal, and shattered dreams. How did I survive? I made the choice to forgive, love, persevere, pray, and praise Him. I have many scars, and some of the battles are still going, but my mindset is different. My threshold to endure is greater because of Him Who lives in and through me.

Prayer: Father, we praise You for our journey. Thank You for being with us through times of great struggle. You have trained me how to endure, persevere, and believe, even in times when I could not see the end. In all things, I will give You thanks and Praise Your holy and mighty Name, Lord Jesus. Amen!

Bonus Encounter

New Direction

FOR ANY OF US to make long-lasting changes, we need to trust Christ to live through us. When we choose to do things God's way and follow His plans, we have the help of the Holy Spirit.

So, are you willing to ask the Holy Spirit how you should implement the changes He wants you to make in your life? Be ready to write them down. Also, be prepared that this may be when He tells you it is time to lay down some of your fleshly desires—the ones that have held you captive. Maybe you have been trying to open a door that He does not want to open. Or maybe you have become complacent in your walk with Christ.

Do you already know some areas you need to lay at Jesus' feet?

_____

_____

_____

_____

_____

Are you ready to let Him be Lord over every area of your life and receive complete freedom?

_____

_____

_____

The Word says,

> *When I was a child, I spoke like a child, I thought like a child. I reasoned like a child. When I became a man, I gave up childish ways.* (1 Cor. 13:11 ESV)

We must all come to a point where we make better choices in certain areas of our lives. The truth is, you already know how much better your life would be if you completely depended on Jesus and His Word. Your soul, mind, will, and emotions, would be renewed and transformed. Freedom and His peace would consume you. Can you imagine? Time is ticking, and seasons are changing. God has a wonderful plan for your life! It's time you experienced it.

Prayer: Father, I choose today that we will make the choice today to put away all childish things and accept responsibility for our actions. I choose to be intentional in this season to pray, meditate on Your Word, and worship Your *Holy Name*. Lord, we need You to give us vision, to renew and refresh our souls so that we can do as it says in Isaiah 40:31, *"But they who wait upon the Lord shall renew their strength; they shall mount up with wings like eagles; they shall not be weary; they shall walk and not faint."* Let us run daily with purpose and calling in this season. Amen.

Scriptures for Meditation

"For the eyes of The Lord are on the righteous, and His ears are open to their prayer. But the face of The Lord is against those who do evil." (1 Pet. 3:12)

"For his eyes are on the ways of a man, and he sees all his steps." (Job 34:21)

"'Relax, Daniel,' he continued, 'don't be afraid. From the moment you decided to humble yourself to receive under-standing, your prayer was heard, and I set out to come to you. But I was waylaid by the angel-prince of the kingdom of Persia and was delayed for a good three weeks. But then Michael, one of the chief angel-princes, intervened to help me. I left him there with the prince of the kingdom of Persia. And now I'm here to help you.'" (Dan. 10:12–14a MSG)

"So, let God work his will in you. Yell a loud no to the devil and watch him scamper. Say a quiet yes to God, and He'll be there in no time. Quit dabbling in sin. Purify your inner life. Quit playing the field. Hit bottom and cry your eyes out. The fun and games are over. Get serious, really serious. Get down on your knees before the Master; it's the only way you'll get on your feet." (Jas. 7:4–10 MSG)

"God, get me out of here, away from this evil; protect me from these vicious people. All they do is think up new ways to be bad; they spend their days plotting war games. They practice the sharp rhetoric of hate and hurt, speak venomous words that maim and kill. God, keep me out of the clutch of these wicked ones, protect me from these vicious people; stuffed with self-importance, they plot ways to trip me up, determined to bring me down. These crooks invent traps to catch me and do their best to incriminate me. I prayed, 'God, you're my God! Listen, God! Mercy! God, my Lord, Strong Savior, protect me when the fighting breaks out! Don't let the wicked have their way, God, don't give them an inch!'" (Ps. 140:1–8 MSG)

"For his eyes are on the ways of a man, and he sees all his steps." (Job 34:21)

"For the eyes of The Lord are on the righteous, and His ears are open to their prayer. But the face of The Lord is against those who do evil." (1 Pet. 3:12)

"…at the Name of Jesus every knee will bow—in heaven and on earth and under the earth…" (Phil. 2:10 NET)

"So then, submit yourselves to God. Resist the Devil, and he will run away from you." (Jas. 4:7 GNT)

"So do not fear, for I am with you; do not be dismayed, for I am your God. I will strengthen you and help you; I will uphold you with my righteous right hand." (Isa. 41:10)

"For I know the plans I have for you," declares the LORD, "plans to prosper you and not to harm you, plans to give you hope and a future." (Jer. 29:11)

"Therefore, if anyone is in Christ, he is a new creation. The old has passed away; behold, the new has come." (2 Cor. 5:17 ESV)

"But whoever drinks of the water that I will give him shall never thirst; but the water that I will give him will become in him a well of water springing up to eternal life." (John 4:4)

"He who believes in Me, as the Scripture said, 'From his innermost being will flow rivers of living water.'" (John 7:38)

"When I was a child, I spoke like a child, I thought like a child. I reasoned like a child. When I became a man, I gave up childish ways." (1 Cor. 13:11 ESV)

"For though we walk in the flesh, we do not war according to the flesh. For the weapons of our warfare are not carnal but mighty in God for pulling down strongholds, casting down arguments and every high thing that exalts itself against the knowledge of God, bringing every thought into captivity to the obedience of Christ." (2 Cor. 10:3–5)

"Although I have the desire to do what is right, I don't do it. I don't do the good I want to do. Instead, I do the evil that I don't want to do. Now, when I do what I don't want to do, I am no longer the one who is doing it. The sin that lives in me is doing it. I take pleasure in God's standards in my inner being; … However, I see a different standard at work throughout my body. It is at war with the standards my mindsets and tries to take me captive to sin's standards which still exist throughout my body. What a miserable person I am! Who will rescue me from my dying body? I thank

God that our Lord Jesus Christ rescues me!" (Rom. 7:18b–20; 23–26 GW)

"Old things have passed away, and all things are become new." (2 Cor. 5:17)

"So here's what I want you to do, God helping you: Take your everyday, ordinary life—your sleeping, eating, going-to-work, and walking-around life—and place it before God as an offering. Embracing what God does for you is the best thing you can do for him. Don't become so well-adjusted to your culture that you fit into it without even thinking. Instead, fix your attention on God. You'll be changed from the inside out. Readily recognize what he wants from you and quickly respond to it. Unlike the culture around you, always dragging you down to its level of immaturity, God brings the best out of you, develops well-formed maturity in you." (Rom. 12:1–2 MSG)

"But I thank God, who always leads us in victory because of Christ. Wherever we go, God uses us to make clear what it means to know Christ. It's like a fragrance that fills the air." (2 Cor. 2:14 GW)

"That's why we can be so sure that every detail in our lives of love for God is worked into something good." (Rom. 8:28 MSG)

"My brothers and sisters, think of the various tests you encounter as occasions for joy. After all, you know that the testing of your faith produces endurance. Let this endurance complete its work so that you may fully mature, be complete, and lack in nothing. But anyone who needs wisdom should ask God, whose very nature is to give to everyone without a second thought, without keeping score. Wisdom will certainly be given to those who ask. Whoever asks shouldn't hesitate. They should ask in faith, without doubting. Whoever doubts is like the surf of the sea, tossed and turned by the wind. People like that should never imagine that they will receive anything from the Lord. They are double-minded, unstable in all their ways. Brothers and sisters who are poor should find satisfaction in their low status because they will die off like the wildflowers. The sun rises with its scorching heat and dries up the grass so that its flowers fall and its beauty is lost. Just like that, in the midst of their daily lives, the wealthy will waste away. Those who stand firm during testing are blessed. They are tried and true. They will receive the life God has promised to those who love him as their reward." (Jas. 1:2–12 CEB)

"Call upon Me in the day of trouble; I shall rescue you, and you will honor Me." (Ps. 50:15)

"Cease striving and know that I am God." (Ps. 46:10b)

"Peace I leave with you. My peace I give to you. I give to you not as the world gives. Don't be troubled or afraid." (John 14:27 CEB)

"I have stored up your word in my heart, that I might not sin against you." (Ps. 119:11 ESV)

"Put off your old self, which belongs to your former manner of life and is corrupt through deceitful desires, and to be renewed in the spirit of your minds, and to put on the new self, created after the likeness of God in true righteousness and holiness." (Eph. 4:22–24 ESV)

"I will take a stand at my watch post and station myself on the tower, and look out to see what he will say to me, and what I will answer concerning my complaint." (Hab. 2:1 ESV)

"My little children, I am writing these things to you, so that you do not sin. But if anyone does sin, we have an Advocate with the Father, Jesus Christ the Righteous One." (1 John 2:1)

"For who has known the mind of the Lord, so as to advise him? But we have the mind of Christ." (1 Cor. 2:16 NET)

"And you, who were formerly alienated and enemies in your mind by wicked works, yet now He has reconciled in the body of His flesh through death, to present you holy and blameless and above reproach in His sight, if you continue in the faith, grounded and settled, and are not removed from the hope of the gospel, which you have heard, and which was preached to every creature which is under heaven, and of which I, Paul, have become a servant." (Col. 1:21–23)

"This is no afternoon athletic contest that we'll walk away from and forget about in a couple of hours. This is for keeps, a life-or-death fight to the finish against the Devil and all his angels. Be prepared. You're up against far more than you can handle on your own. Take all the help you can get, every weapon God has issued, so that when it's all over but the shouting you'll still be on your feet. Truth, righteousness, peace, faith, and salvation are more than words. Learn how to apply them. You'll need them throughout your life. God's Word is an indispensable weapon. In the same way, prayer is essential in this ongoing warfare. Pray hard and long. Pray for your brothers and sisters. Keep your eyes open. Keep each other's spirits up so that no one falls behind or drops out." (Eph. 6:11–18 MSG)

"And the God of all grace, who called you to his eternal glory in Christ, after you have suffered a little while, will himself restore you and make you strong, firm, and steadfast." (1 Pet. 5:10 NIV)

"For the Word of God is alive and active, sharper than any double-edged sword, it penetrates even to dividing soul and spirit, joints and marrow; it judges the thoughts attitudes of the heart. Nothing in all creation is hidden from God's sight. Everything is uncovered and laid bare before the eyes of him to whom we must give account." (Heb. 4:12–13 NIV)

"Since then we have a great high priest who has passed through the heavens. Jesus, the Son of God, let us hold fast our confession. For we do not have a high priest who is unable to sympathize with our weakness, but one who in every respect has been tempted as we are, yet without sin. Let us then with confidence draw near to the throne of grace, that we may receive mercy and find grace to help in the time of need." (Heb. 4:14)

"But seek first the Kingdom of God and his righteousness, and all these things will be added to you." (Matt. 6:33 ESV)